Praise for Called by God

"God calls each one of us to lives of extraordinary holiness; our task is to prepare for his call, and to respond with generosity, as the Blessed Mother did. *Called by God* draws from the best spiritual wisdom of the Church to help young women hear the Lord, and respond in freedom, generosity, and joy. This is an invaluable and beautiful book for young women discerning and preparing for religious life."

Most Reverend James D. Conley
Bishop of Lincoln, Nebraska

"Anyone considering vocational life should see this masterpiece of information holding every aspect of what one might need to know about religious life when considering this call. Going back through the history of saints and popes we are led to understand every possible approach to the subject. If you have any desire to be a religious sister or brother or priest, or to marry with the Church's blessing, don't hesitate to read this amazing book. If I had, I am certain I would enter Regina Laudis!"

Mother Dolores Hart
Abbey of Regina Laudis, Bethlehem, Connecticut

"How refreshing, how utterly right, that a Catholic wife and mother should help young women discern vocations to the religious life! After all, as the Catechism tells us, 'esteem of virginity for the sake of the Kingdom and the Christian understanding of marriage are inseparable, and they reinforce each other.' With the admirable clarity of its language, the sense it conveys to the reader of being personally addressed, and the abundant references to the lives of the saints, Rachael Collins' new book will become, I am sure, a little classic of contemporary Catholic spirituality."

FR. JOHN SAWARD
Author and Blackfriars Lecturer, Oxford University

"Every young woman owes it to herself to discern whether she is being called to religious life. As Collins beautifully shows with her own journey, supported by the testimonies of the saints and the few others who have written well on the subject, discernment itself is a spiritually enriching process, even if one is ultimately called to married life. Opening oneself to God's grace in the practical and reflective ways Collins suggests will only help a young woman to be the wife, mother, daughter of God, and, indeed, saint that she is called to be."

AURORA GRIFFIN
Author, *How I Stayed Catholic at Harvard: 40 Tips for Faithful College Students*

"There are so few solid books for young women discerning religious life in the Catholic Church these days. Rachael Marie Collins has amassed a wealth of good information and wisdom that will guide women as they seek the will of God. As a married woman and mother, who seriously considered religious life herself, the author will be invaluable to those who may be called to be a Bride of Christ!"

Fr. Brett Brannen
Author of *To Save a Thousand Souls: A Guide for Discerning a Vocation to Diocesan Priesthood* and *A Priest in the Family: A Guide for Parents Whose Sons are Considering Priesthood*

"Here is a book that fills an important gap with sound advice for young women about how to discern a religious vocation. The fruit of much careful study of Catholic tradition as well as personal experience, this book is chock full of helpful reflections. I especially enjoyed the section on the need for good friendships—friendships with the Saints, with those wise in matters of the spiritual life, and with like-minded people of one's own age."

Fr. Joseph Koterski, S.J.,
Professor of Philosophy, Fordham University

"Rachael Marie Collins has created a rare aid for those considering to step out into the realm of poverty, chastity, and obedience as a consecrated religious. This calling has always had a mystery about it, but now even more. Rachel Marie Collins gets a conversation going within the deepest heart of the one who is wondering, 'What if?' We need good Catholic married people, priests, and consecrated men and women in our Church family. This beautiful book is a gift from one part of the family to another to encourage women to listen, wonder and not to be afraid."

MOTHER MARY ELIZABETH KLOSS
St. Scholastica Priory, Petersham, Massachusetts

"This excellent volume touches on every aspect of the discernment process, drawing from a rich theological tradition including Teresa of Ávila, Edith Stein, Mother Teresa, and many others. An invaluable companion for all women contemplating religious life."

MOST REVEREND ANTHONY COLIN FISHER
Archbishop of Sydney, Australia

CALLED
BY GOD

CALLED
BY GOD

DISCERNMENT *and* PREPARATION
for RELIGIOUS LIFE

RACHAEL MARIE COLLINS

EMMAUS
ROAD
PUBLISHING

Steubenville, Ohio
www.EmmausRoad.org

For my children and their much-loved nanny,
Marie Therese.

This printing was funded by a donation made in Memory of Mr. & Mrs. Harold Ziegler

Emmaus Road Publishing
1468 Parkview Circle
Steubenville, Ohio 43952

Library of Congress Cataloging-in-Publication Data
Names: Collins, Rachael Marie, 1978- author.
Title: Called by God : discernment and preparation for religious life /
Rachael Marie Collins.
Description: Steubenville : Emmaus Road Pub., 2017.
Identifiers: LCCN 2017020423 (print) | LCCN 2017019404 (ebook) | ISBN
9781945125577 (hardcover) | ISBN 9781945125492 (pbk.) | ISBN
9781945125508 (ebook)
Subjects: LCSH: Monastic and religious life of women. | Monasticism and
religious orders for women. | Spiritual life--Catholic Church. |
Vocation--Catholic Church.
Classification: LCC BX4210 .C545 2017 (ebook) | LCC BX4210 (print) | DDC
248.8/9432--dc23
LC record available at https://lccn.loc.gov/2017020423

Cover image: *The Annunciation*, by Fra Filippo Lippi, ca. 1449–59,
National Gallery, London, U.K.
Cover design and layout by Margaret Ryland

Table of Contents

Foreword	xv
Acknowledgments	xxi
Introduction	xxv
Part I: Discernment	1
Discernment as Courtship	3
Preparation as Discernment	9
A Supernatural Vocation	13
A Superior Way of Life	17
Vocare: "To Call" and "To Name"	29
Stages of Formation: Room for Error	35
Discerning That You Are Not Called to Religious Life	37
A Universal Call to Sanctity	41
Spiritual Motherhood	47
Part II: Preparation	53
Spiritual Direction	55
The Spiritual Life	59
The Mechanics	67
Prayer	67
Participation in the Sacraments	71
Adoration	72
Silence	72
Mortification	75
Annual Retreat	78
Fulfillment of Duties of State	78
Obedience	79
Study	80

Service 83

Table 1: The Spiritual and Corporal Works of Mercy 84

Ascending the Mountain 89

Illustration 1: Climbing the Mountain of God 91

Evil 93

The Tabernacle of Your Heart and Home 97

Keep Good Company 101

Dating 105

Discretion 109

Modesty 113

Hostile Environments 117

Humiliations 121

Dominant Defect 125

The Little Way of the Sinner:
Offering God Our Failures 129

The Magdalene: Healing and Conversion 133

First Front: Spiritual Healing 137

Second Front: Emotional Healing 138

Fear of Suffering 141

Expiation 145

Evangelization through Love 147

Asking for Signs 155

Some Practical Matters 157

Debt 158

Investigate 158

Some Additional Considerations 161

Impediments 161

Exceptions 163

Homesickness 163

Parental and Sibling Grief 164

Parental Resistance	167
Pilgrimages and Mission Trips	168
Martyrdom	173
Expectations	177
Sentimentality	181
Competition and Humility	183
Prayer for Perseverance	187
Quagmires and Endgames	191
Do Not Delay	195
Appendix: Signs of a Vocation	199

"A call can't be explained any more than you can explain falling in love." Mother Benedict Duss, the first Abbess and foundress of the Benedictine Abbey of Regina Laudis in Bethlehem, Connecticut, explained vocation this way many years ago to my friend Richard DeNeut. As a non-Catholic, he struggled to understand the idea of "a call." Even faithful Catholics, however, sometimes struggle to truly understand what it is to have a vocation. Lady Abbess' analogy has stuck with me as one of the most apt explanations for what it is to be called, particularly for my own call to religious life. Really, it is more than just an analogy—a vocation is falling in love. It is a discovery of the fullest love that encompasses all others.

Some young women reading this might already have an idea that this is true. Perhaps you have already discovered that nothing in your present life will fulfill you as you are called to be fulfilled.

But many other young women may be more like myself. If someone had told me at seventeen that someday I would become a cloistered nun, I never would have believed them. I never wanted to enter a monastery. From a very young age, my greatest desire was to become an actress. I wanted to go to Hollywood with my father and be like the star Gene Tierney.

Both my father and my mother had dreams of becoming Hollywood actors. My father moved to California to be in films, and my mother and I followed him quickly. I grew up watching films through the projector window with my grandfather at the movie house in Chicago, where I lived during the school year with my grandparents. It was in the movie house, where my grandfather worked as a projectionist, that I first decided I wanted to be an actress. And in 1957, at nineteen, I starred in my first film, *Loving You*, alongside Elvis Presley. It was the start of doing everything I had always wanted to do.

However, I have realized that a vocation isn't necessarily something you've always wanted to do. It's something you're called to. And I was called by God.

Lest I scare anyone into running further from her vocation, let me say that God did not force me to give up my dreams in order to enter the convent. He didn't force me to run away from the world. He just led me to enter it in a more profound way.

After starring in another film with Elvis, I spent nine months in 1959 on Broadway in *The Pleasure of His Company*, with a packed schedule that left me exhausted. One of my friends suggested that I visit a nice monastery she knew of in Connecticut where I could take some time away from work. At first I didn't want to go anywhere near nuns. But when she assured me that I could just stay in their guest house for a rest, I agreed to go.

Stepping onto the monastery grounds for the first time, I felt instinctively that this was where I was called to be. It's something I couldn't explain, but that needed no explanation. When I asked Mother Benedict if she thought someone like me could be called to the monastery, she told me, "No, Dolores, return to Hollywood and continue your career."

And despite my feeling that the abbey—at the time just a small monastery—was the place for me, I couldn't have been happier to hear her advice. I left as fast as I could and went back to making movies. I returned to my friends in Hollywood and even got engaged to one of my very best friends, Don Robinson.

But the feeling that I was called to return to the abbey never left me. As I was on the verge of marrying the man I loved and signing a seven-year contract with MGM, I still couldn't forget Regina Laudis. I stayed in contact with Lady Abbess, exchanging letters through the years.

One night in 1963, Don and I went to a party celebrating our engagement. On the way home, Don suddenly stopped the car. He asked, "Dolores, what's wrong? You weren't at the party tonight. I just need you to tell me you love me."

I did love him. But it wasn't the same as the love that called me to Regina Laudis. I could no longer deny that call.

It was hard for my friends and family to understand, just as it's hard for others who hear my story now. I had everything I had ever wanted, with the promise of further success and happiness. This, I think, is what people find the hardest to grasp—how someone who had all that earthly happiness could give it up. But I never looked at it like that. While those first years in religious life were difficult, I never felt that I had been cheated out of a dream. I simply felt that I had fallen in love, and that I would do anything to follow that love.

Nor was I running away from Hollywood or fame. I loved acting, and I still believe that films have a powerful opportunity to share important truths with the entire world in a special way. I did not leave Hollywood out of fear, just as any young woman should not seek religious life as an escape. My vocation as a nun was trading one good for a higher good—my will for God's will.

That does not mean my vocation has always been easy. The first seven years in the abbey were particularly difficult. But I chose to answer God's call to religious life, just as I chose to become a Catholic when I was ten years old, and just as I chose to remain faithful to my conscience throughout my time in Hollywood despite many challenges.

We each have an important vocation. Whether we are called to religious life or not, we are each created with a very specific purpose.

Today there is a depth of suffering, of non-being, that I am saddened to see whenever I travel from the abbey. Now, more than ever before, many people, young and old, don't know who they are, and young people face this difficulty with more frequency, I believe. We are told to reach for things outside of ourselves to cut across the feeling of emptiness. However, nothing in the outside world will fill the longing each of has to discover the person we were created to be.

The Rule of St. Benedict begins with one of my favorite quotes, and I believe it is just as important now as it was when it was written 1,500 years ago, if not more so. It begins: "Listen carefully, my son, to the master's instructions, and attend to them with the ear of your heart."

God wishes to speak to us in our innermost heart. We will not find fulfillment only in our accomplishments, achievements, or successes. If we have not taken the time to listen carefully with the ear of the heart and discern what our true calling is, we will not experience life—or love—to its fullest.

Young people today are at a disadvantage in a certain sense because they have not been taught how to listen with the ear of the heart. In addition, there is so much noise in the world calling for their attention that it is difficult to listen closely enough to hear the one true call.

This is one reason why fewer young women are entering religious life now than at any time before. Young women need encouragement to cut through the noise distracting them from listening to their own hearts.

I believe this book will give young women the encouragement and the wisdom they need to grow in their discernment. Just as I needed Lady Abbess' wise advice to guide me through my discernment, young women need someone to guide them through the process in order to discern well. Rachael Collins offers all young women sage advice that will help them truly listen with the ear of their heart, whether they are called to religious life or not.

We each have something special within us that we can give to the world. Finding our calling gives us the deepest life we can live. Helping young women discover this is one of the greatest gifts we can give, as well as one of our greatest responsibilities.

MOTHER DOLORES HART, OSB
The Epiphany of the Lord 2019

Acknowledgments

First acknowledgement is owed to my beloved husband, Kevin. Thank you for your encouragement, editing, and patience!

Thank you also to Marie Therese, Bernadette, Anna Gawley, Msgr. Victor Martinez, Fr. Sean Kopczynski, M.S.J.B., Fr. Matthew MacDonald, Fr. Michael Manz, Sr. Mary Ephrem, O.P., Sr. Maravillas, O.C.D., Fr. Anthony Baetzold, C.F.R., Kathryn Cooper, Fergal Martin and all the staff at Catholic Truth Society, Priscilla McCaffrey, Roger McCaffrey, Aurora Griffin, Chris Erickson, and all the staff at Emmaus Road Publishing.

And just so, He has called women in all times to the most intimate union with Him: they are to be emissaries of His love, proclaimers of His will to kings and popes, and forerunners of His Kingdom in the hearts of men. To be the *Spouse of Christ* is the most sublime vocation which has been given, and whosoever sees this way open before her will yearn for no other way.

Saint Edith Stein

Introduction

Easter Week 2015
Year for Consecrated Life

This book was written in 2015 (the Year for Consecrated Life) as a series of letters to our babysitter, Marie Therese, who felt that God might be calling her to religious life. She was just starting the discernment process and when I couldn't find any books to accompany her on this journey, I wrote down some thoughts and suggestions.

It must seem presumptuous for me as a married woman to write about discernment and preparation for religious life. I do not know religious life but I do know what it is to discern and I do know what it is to be (and remain!) a beginner in the spiritual life. These letters are based on my own discernment which started at thirteen and continued, on and off, until I was twenty-three.

In these letters, I eschew the modern approach, which encourages young women to focus on their subjective and inconsistent feelings and desires. Rather, I argue, the way to discern religious life is to *prepare for it*: to slowly enter into the spiritual life by establishing a life of prayer and mortification so that one understands and tastes the "work" of a religious before one enters.

My secondary aim is to guide the reader to richer, more formidable authors and resources that she can delve into as needed. Some of these authors are modern; many are from our past. All contribute to the rich spiritual tradition of the Church.

I rely heavily on the writing and witness of our saintly sisters in Christ—women who understood and embodied what Saint John Paul II called our "feminine genius" (*Mulieris dignitatem*)—Saint Teresa of Ávila, Saint Thérèse of Lisieux, Saint Faustina, Saint Teresa Benedicta of the Cross, Saint Teresa of the Andes, Saint Elizabeth of the Trinity, and Saint Teresa of Calcutta, to name but a few. They provide compelling witness to the joy and beauty of religious life.

The reader might find some of what I suggest difficult, somewhat serious, and rather challenging. Christ does challenge us, yes. But He also invites us—in whatever state of life He intends for us—to joyful union with Him; *He makes possible* a life richer and more fulfilling than any we can imagine for ourselves.

Older religious might be reminded of their own formation. Why, they might ask, would these younger generations embrace a spirituality that is so exacting? Because nothing less than a full gift of self—whether that be in marriage or religious life—will satisfy! Nothing less than an offering of our all—even though we know that in trying for the ideal of Christ, we will inevitably stumble—will quench the desires of our heart (Ps 37:3–7).

Fortunately, Christ meets us in our failures and it is only when we offer all of ourselves to Him—the broken bits as well as the whole bits—the failures as well as our successes—that He can transform us into our true selves: radiant daughters of God. It is a rigorous way of life, but with humility, perseverance, and grace, you'll also find it joyful and beautiful.

I hope this book is helpful to young women discerning

whether to enter the convent. I also hope it will assist fathers, mothers, siblings, and priests in supporting their daughters, sisters, and parishioners as they progress towards spiritual union with Christ.

In the meantime, please know that I am praying (and making little sacrifices) for all the young women who read this book. I pray that God does call you to religious life and that you'll have the courage to enter. I pray that you'll flourish as you discern and experience great peace as you joyfully live out your religious vocation.

Part I:
Vocation and Discernment

DISCERNMENT AS COURTSHIP

Dear Marie Therese,

Don't be disheartened that you still aren't sure what God is asking of you. It can take a long time to discern a call to religious life.

Part of the problem is that you haven't been taught how to discern. It is difficult to accomplish something when you don't know where to start or how to proceed.

Some souls know from a very early age that they are called to belong to Him and to Him alone.[1] Saint Faustina knew at age seven and first sought entry into the religious life at eighteen. Saint Thérèse of Lisieux, your namesake, also knew from an early age and first tried to enter Carmel at age fourteen. It is more common to spend many years in discernment.[2] It took Saint Thérèse's parents many years to discern that they were *not* called to religious life. Saints Zélie and Louis Martin were told at ages twenty and twenty-two, respectively, that they did not have a vocation to religious life, despite yearning for such a life for many years. Louis remained single for nearly fifteen years before marrying Zélie in 1858 at age thirty-five. Zélie was twenty-nine.

Saint John Neumann's discernment was also lengthy. He

---

[1] In the tradition of Saint Teresa of Ávila, Saint Thérèse of Lisieux, and so on, I use the term "soul" to describe the person and her engagement in the spiritual life. This is not meant to suggest or endorse a dualistic vision of the human person.

[2] Saint Augustine, Saint Francis of Assisi, Saint Francis Xavier, among many others, are examples.

had wanted to study medicine and wasn't planning on entering the seminary at all until his mother convinced him to apply.[3] After he entered the seminary, all ordinations in his native Bohemia were put on hold. He became a priest only after he emigrated from Bohemia to the United States, where there was a need for German-speaking priests.[4]

While it may be frustrating that you cannot clearly see what path you are called to take, do not be discouraged! The cross of unknowing can be a great gift.

This time of discernment is really a period of preparation and training—preparation for and training in the religious life. For this is how one discerns.

It is also a period of courtship. Throughout this stage of discernment, Jesus desires you for Himself and wants to draw you closer to Himself, to teach you to love Him.

During a Christian courtship, people discern whether they should marry. They learn about one another. They develop ways and patterns of speaking with and relating to one another. They also help one another with acts of love and service. As they discern together, they slowly and prudently start to lay a foundation for marriage.

Your courtship with Christ is no different. Get to know Him. Spend regular time with Him in prayer. Develop a way of relating to Him and being with Him. Allow Him into your heart. Allow Him to court you and love you.

In the same way that a woman will allow her fiancé to lift something heavy for her or perhaps help her father with a repair around the house or some other manly work, allow

---

3 Philip Douglas, *Saint of Philadelphia: The Life of Bishop John Neumann* (Cambridge, MA: Ravengate, 1977), 27.

4 Ibid.

Jesus as your betrothed or possible future spouse to do much for you. You do not have to do the heavy lifting by yourself anymore. He is waiting for your permission to help you.

If you are willing, Jesus will shower your soul with many graces during this period of discernment. Your discernment period is a time to draw closer to God. It is a time to develop a rich interior life so that you: (a) are ready to enter religious life if called; or (b) can continue with life in the world in a solid and holy way, should it be God's will that you serve Him as a layperson.

The desire to give oneself entirely to Christ is a grace from Jesus. Even if you are not called to religious life, it pleases Him that you are sincere in seeking out His will for you and trying to conform to it.

Ask Jesus to give you the grace to endure this wait patiently. In moments of difficulty or impatience, meditate on Christ's hidden life—the life He led from birth to age thirty.[5]

For thirty years He knew who He was and what He was to do for us, and yet He waited all that time. He spent this time honoring, loving, and assisting His mother, Mary, and His adoptive father, Saint Joseph, praying, practicing His carpentry trade, and diligently fulfilling all His duties of state.[6]

Here you have the perfect model to follow. Ask Jesus of the hidden life to help you use this time of discernment and preparation well. Try to be productive and intentional in how you live during this wait. It is given to you to prepare: pray, read and study, attend Holy Mass, practice prudent and

---

[5] Christ's public life was from age thirty until His death at age thirty-three.

[6] Christ fulfilled the duties of state associated with His life as a child and young adult perfectly. See the section "Fulfillment of Duties of State" beginning on p. 78 for more on this topic.

thoughtful obedience (to your parents and confessor), and grow in a life of regular prayer and the sacraments.

Like Christ, live frugally. Like Christ, behave, dress, and speak modestly. Like Christ, support your family. Like Christ, fulfill all your duties of state. Like Christ, devote yourself to prayer and the diligent study of Sacred Scripture and the Catholic faith. Like Christ, engage in disciplined work. Above all, be joyful. You have been given a grace to discern. Our Lord is inviting you closer to Him, no matter what He decides for you.

God will also use the discernment period to reveal areas in which you need to grow. Some souls might need to overcome the faults of impatience and self-absorption. Others might need to grow in forbearance, fidelity, or courage.

Saint Faustina, for example, allowed her parents' opposition to deter her from entering the convent. "Interiorly," she "shunned God" and "tried . . . to stifle it [the incessant call of grace] with amusements." Jesus rebuked her in a vision. He said to her, "How long shall I put up with you and how long will you keep putting me off?"[7]

Saint Faustina begged Jesus for the grace to know what to do. When He revealed what this was, she took decisive and immediate action. She left home and traveled immediately to Warsaw as instructed by Our Lord. Jesus gave her the grace to overcome her timidity.

From all accounts, Saint John Vianney struggled as a student. He was bright and pious, but unable to sufficiently master Latin to pass his exams for the priesthood. After an-

---

[7] Saint Maria Faustina Kowalska, *Diary: Divine Mercy in My Soul*, 3rd ed. (Stockbridge, MA: Marian Press, 2005), nos. 9–10.

other failed attempt he went on pilgrimage to beg assistance from Our Lady. Only then was he successful.[8]

The responses of Saint John Vianney and Saint Faustina illustrate how we should approach obstacles, trials, or weaknesses uncovered during the discernment period. Take the matter to Our Lord and Our Lady, and ask for their assistance.

Do not think that you can do this by yourself. Most souls at this stage—although not all—are beginners in the spiritual life. They are novices. Don't be disheartened. Most of the great saints still had more growth, more suffering to endure, and more sanctity to obtain when they entered into their vocations.[9]

Beg God for the graces you need to overcome any faults He reveals to you during this period of courtship. Specifically request the graces of perseverance, patience, purity, humility, courage, fidelity, and wisdom. Ask Our Lady to intercede on your behalf. Visit Him often in the Blessed Sacrament and ask Him for the assistance you need.

---

[8] George W. Rutler, *The Cure D'Ars Today: St. John Vianney* (San Francisco: Ignatius, 1988), 67, 82–87.

[9] Saint Teresa of the Andes is a possible exception.

Preparation as Discernment

Dear Marie Therese,

The best way to discern whether you are called to religious life is to *prepare* for religious life. In the same way that an athlete prepares for a competition, or a student for university study, you can begin readying yourself now for religious life.

When Saint Thomas More discerned whether he should become a priest, he did so by engaging in "exercises of piety, looking to and pondering on the priesthood in vigils, fasts, and prayers, and similar austerities."[10] In other words, his discernment was a form of preparation—he entered deeply into the spiritual life and, in doing so, obtained an answer as to his vocation.

His biographer notes that the saint was more thoroughly prepared for the priesthood than most candidates who do enter. Not knowing whether he had the strength to live chastely, Saint Thomas More followed the advice of Saint Paul (1 Cor 7) and entered into marriage: "The one thing that prevented him from giving himself to that kind of life was that he could not shake off the desire of the married state. He chose, therefore, to be a chaste husband rather than an impure priest."[11]

Saint Teresa of the Andes also discerned through preparation. She entered the Carmel of Los Andes in Chile at age nineteen, having spent four or more years preparing for reli-

---

[10] Thomas Edward Bridgett, *Life and Writings of Blessed Thomas More: Lord Chancellor of England and Martyr Under Henry VIII* (London: Burns, Oates & Washbourne, 1924), 23.

[11] Ibid.

gious life. On her fifteenth birthday, she wrote that "the future hasn't been revealed to me, yet Jesus has pulled back the curtain and I have glimpsed the beautiful shores of Carmel."[12] She "embarked on a very structured prayer life,"[13] through which she strove to be a "Carmelite in the world."[14]

During this time, Teresa often experienced great dryness and aridity in her prayer life. Nevertheless, she attended daily Mass, spent time in prayer, dutifully fulfilled her obligations as a student, served others with love, and cheerfully made sacrifices for the conversion of sinners. She considered herself "betrothed" to Jesus and offered gifts of sacrifice and prayer to Him as part of their courtship:

> Every sacrifice made is small compared with the value of one soul. God gave His life for them, yet how we disregard their salvation. As one betrothed to Him, I must thirst for souls, and offer my Espoused the bloodshed for each of them. And how can we win these souls? Prayer, mortification and suffering.[15]

She did this so well that when she did enter religious life, Our Lord kept her in Carmel for a mere ten months before calling her to heaven. She died having scaled the uppermost heights of sanctity.

Follow the examples of Saint Thomas More and Saint Teresa of the Andes. If you feel an attraction for the religious

---

[12] Jennifer Moorcroft, *God is All Joy: The Life of St. Teresa of the Andes* (Washington, DC: ICS Publications, 2009), 23.

[13] Ibid., 27.

[14] Ibid., 47.

[15] Ibid., 32.

life or wonder whether it might be for you, then prepare for it. Act as if you are called. Say a prayer of obstruction[16] and take the first steps toward entering.[17]

This type of discernment allows you to combine prayerful contemplation and reflection with necessary action. Discernment should not be restricted to passive introspection. This can lead to self-absorption and inaction. Rather, it is wise to take a number of preparatory steps in your discernment and to then reflect and pray on the fruit of these steps. Ask yourself: "Did that step bring me peace? What was the fruit? Did any good come of this?"

In so doing you move beyond simply asking "am I called?" to considering questions such as, "where will my talents and life best be of use in the service of others?" In this way, your discernment shifts from being self-focused to other-focused, from internal to external, from emotions to action. Paradoxically, this outward movement in your reflections will facilitate greater clarity when you do consider the internal movements within your soul.[18]

Approaching discernment in this way will help you remain peaceful and detached. Try to be detached about your

---

[16] Something like this: *Dear Jesus, if You do not want me to be a religious, please do not allow me to enter the convent. Allow me to be rejected or deterred in some way. If You do wish me to enter, then please allow and facilitate it. Also pray for the grace to love your vocation, whatever that might be.*

[17] "Diligent discernment" is another term used to describe this type of discernment; see Brett A. Brannen, *To Save a Thousand Souls: A Guide for Discerning a Vocation to Diocesan Priesthood* (Valdosta, GA: Vianney Vocations, 2010), 157–158.

[18] This approach combines the type of discernment recommended by Saint Ignatius of Loyola with that preferred by Saint Thomas Aquinas. See Joseph Bolin, Paths Of Love: The Discernment Of Vocation According To Aquinas, Ignatius, And Pope John Paul II (CreateSpace Independent Publishing Platform, 2008).

need for certainty. When you ask Him for light regarding your vocation, He hears you and He will respond. Perhaps not when you want Him to respond, but He will do so in His time. He *will* guide you in this.

Pray to God for the strength, wisdom, and generosity to get on with the task of preparing for and entering religious life. And then start. There is nothing more important than this. Do not be afraid. It will become clear if you do not have a vocation to religious life.

READING LIST

Discernment
+ William Doyle, *Vocations*
+ Stephano M. Manelli, *Come and Follow Me*
+ Clare Matthiass, *Discerning Religious Life*

Preparation
+ Francis de Sales, *Introduction to the Devout Life*

Detachment
+ Jean-Pierre de Caussade, S.J., *Abandonment to Divine Providence*
+ Jacques Philippe, *Searching for and Maintaining Peace: A Small Treatise on Peace of Heart*
+ Jean Baptiste Saint-Jure and Claude de la Colombière, *Trustful Surrender to Divine Providence: The Secret of Peace and Happiness*

A Supernatural Vocation

Dear Marie Therese,

One of the reasons it took me so long to discern my vocation was that I was constantly looking for absolute certainty about whether or not I was called. I was told to consider whether I was "called" but I wasn't sure what that "calling" looked or felt like. I was told to seek out the deepest desires of my heart—that my true vocation would satisfy me in a way that the other options would not. But I wasn't sure how to identify the deepest desires of my heart.

It was extremely difficult for me to discern anything. My confessor *did not* think I had a vocation to religious life. Two mother superiors thought I *probably did* have a vocation. My parish priest was *sure* I was called to religious life. My parents hoped I *didn't* have a vocation. As for me, I was constantly unsure, swinging from one direction to the other in a most undisciplined fashion.

While I really did desire to enter religious life and was willing to enter should it be God's will for me, the methodology I used to discern was seriously flawed. It is unfortunate that the modern approach to discernment encourages young women to focus on their subjective and inconsistent feelings and desires. This is not advisable.

First, our emotions and desires—especially those that are unexamined or superficial—tend to be changeable. They are affected by our imagination and moods. An unpurified, immature imagination, for example, can distort our ability to see things (including ourselves) accurately. This is why it is so important to monitor our intake of media—especially magazines, pop music, and television programs—which can influence the way we feel, imagine, or think about important things such as love, marriage, sex, and God.[19] Overcoming a tendency towards sentimentality will help you with this.[20]

Second, marriage is a *natural* vocation while religious life is a *supernatural* vocation. By this I mean that our *natural* inclination is to want marriage. We tend to desire the companionship and joy a spouse and children can bring. Because it is necessary for a properly ordered civil society, marriage has had a long and widespread existence. Marriage existed before Christ was born; it continues to exist in neo-pagan cultures now.

In other words, marriage doesn't depend on faith in God or a particular, special calling from God in the way that a religious vocation does. Yes, Christ did make marriage a sacrament. It is a beautiful means of obtaining sanctity; but this does not change the fact that marriage is also the *natural default* to which most of us gravitate. It is simply part of how we are built.

The religious life is *naturally* less attractive because it involves a radical death to self from the very beginning. Mar-

---

[19] Be aware of the modern tendency to romanticize romantic love. The culture around you is saturated with the idea that we should aspire to be "in love." By choosing religious life you might think that you're missing out. The type of love marketed to you by pop songs, movies, television shows, magazines, and even operas is not the same as married love. Marriage is more like a marathon than a sprint. The early feelings of infatuation do not last. With the grace of God, this immature love should evolve into something more profound—much deeper and much more stable. It is not, however, the same as the initial infatuation common in courtship and early marriage.

[20] See the chapter in this book titled "Sentimentality."

riage also involves a great death to self—it just happens more slowly and is less obvious at the start. Having a spouse and raising children is hard work. To do it well means much sacrifice and constant self-denial for the sake of others. Even in a happy, Christian marriage, one must endure suffering: we cannot avoid the Cross.

When Saint Teresa of the Andes finished school, she remained at home and helped her mother serve the family and manage the home for several months before entering religious life. She had not expected domestic life to be as taxing as she found it. For her it became a painful form of self-abnegation:

> When I first left school, I thought, Rev. Mother, I'd have a little more free time and that I would write you more often. But just the opposite has happened. Believe me, when I say that I don't have a free moment. Now it's one thing, then another, keeping me constantly occupied. . . . The resolution I made on my retreat was to sacrifice myself for everyone. How much the continuous sacrifice costs at times.[21]

One important consequence of all this is that you can, and sometimes should, choose against the natural inclination to marriage. In other words, a desire for and attraction to marriage doesn't rule out that one is also called to religious life.

Don't give any significance to superficial feelings or desires. When you do examine your feelings and emotions, focus on these two things: (a) your conscience, and (b) which op-

---

[21] Teresa of the Andes to Mother Angelica Teresa, 14 October 1918, *Letters of Saint Teresa of the Andes*, trans. Michael D. Griffin, O.C.D. (Hubertus, WI: Teresian Charism Press, 1994), 67.

tion gives you the greatest sense of peace—not excitement, passion, or short-lived certainty, but peace.

Read *The Discernment of Spirits* by Father Timothy Gallagher, O.M.V., for further instruction and guidance on this part of your discernment process.

READING LIST

+ Brett A. Brannen, *To Save a Thousand Souls: A Guide for Discerning a Vocation to the Diocesan Priesthood*
+ Timothy Gallagher, O.M.V., *The Discernment of Spirits*
+ Timothy Gallagher, O.M.V., *Discerning the Will of God*
+ John Paul II, *The Meaning of Vocation: In the Words of John Paul II*
+ Francis de Sales, *Finding God's Will for You*
+ Abbott William, M.M.A., *A Calling: An Autobiography and the Founding of the Maronite Monks of Adoration*

A Superior Way of Life

Dear Marie Therese,

Nowadays we tend to treat the religious life as a sort of spiritual unicorn for which some special, esoteric invitation is necessary even to consider it. Religious vocations should be a "normal thing in Christian life."[22] The sentiment that it is rare and unusual is at odds with Scripture, the writings of the saints, and the counsel of Saint Thomas Aquinas.

Saint John Bosco reportedly said that one-third of the Catholic population has a religious vocation.[23] Likewise, Saint Paul exhorts those who can enter into religious life to do so. It is, he says, the better way of life: ". . . he who marries his betrothed does well; and he who refrains from marriage will do better" (1 Cor 7:38). Saint Paul is right. Objectively, it *is* the more perfect way of life. It enables the soul to embrace God without the distractions of having to provide and care for a spouse and child. Under such conditions, the soul can progress more rapidly in the spiritual life:

> The unmarried man is anxious about the affairs of
> the Lord, how to please the Lord; but the married
> man is anxious about worldly affairs, how to please
> his wife, and his interests are divided. And the un-

---

[22] Richard Butler, *Religious Vocations: An Unnecessary Mystery* (Charlotte, NC: TAN Books, 1961), 58.

[23] Stephano M. Manelli, *Come and Follow Me* (New Bedford, MA: Franciscans of the Immaculate, 2000), 17. Other reports claim the Saint said that one tenth of the population has religious vocations.

17

married woman or virgin is anxious about the affairs of the Lord, how to be holy in body and spirit; but the married woman is anxious about worldly affairs, how to please her husband. (1 Cor 7:32–34)

Like Saint Paul, Saint Thomas Aquinas also considered religious life to be a "greater good." He describes the religious state as a "spiritual schooling for the attainment of the perfection of charity"[24] and states that: "Thus, it is certain that entrance into religion [religious life] is a greater good, and to doubt about this is to disparage Christ Who gave this counsel."[25]

The Angelic Doctor warns that those who fail to see religious life as an objectively superior good "disparage Christ." This is because the evangelical counsels (also known as the counsels of perfection: poverty, chastity, and obedience) were given to us by Christ and those who choose to live by them (as nuns and religious sisters do) go beyond what is merely necessary for salvation and opt for the way of perfection.[26]

Christ introduces us to the evangelical counsels in Matthew 19. Here Jesus raises the idea of celibacy, telling us that "there are eunuchs who have made themselves eunuchs for the sake of the kingdom of heaven" and that "he who is able to receive this, let him receive it" (Mt 19:12). Those who choose

---

[24] Thomas Aquinas, *Summa Theologica*, trans. Fathers of the English Dominican Province (Notre Dame, IN: Ave Maria Press, 1948), II-II, q. 189, a. 1. Hereafter cited as *ST*.

[25] Ibid., a. 10.

[26] Nun is the title given to a religious woman in an enclosed or cloistered order. A religious sister is a woman who is a member of a semi-active religious order. The distinction comes from the traditional classification of nuns as the "second order" of a religious family. Religious sisters were classified as "third order."

virginity for love of God, He says, are "like angels in heaven" (Mt 22:30).

Later we are told of the rich young man who asks Jesus what he must do to have eternal life (Mt 19:16–30).[27] Our Lord starts by telling the young man to obey the commandments:

> And behold, one came up to him, saying "Teacher, what good deed must I do, to have eternal life?" And he said to him, "Why do you ask me about what is good? One there is who is good. If you would enter life, keep the commandments." He said to him, "Which?" And Jesus said, "You shall not kill, You shall not commit adultery, You shall not steal, You shall not bear false witness, Honor your father and mother, and, You shall love your neighbor as yourself." (Mt 19:16–19)

When the young man responds that he does all this, Our Lord invites him to abandon everything and to follow Him (Mt 19:20–21):

> The young man said to him, "All these I have observed; what do I still lack?" Jesus said to him, "If you would be *perfect*, go, sell what you possess and give to

---

[27] Also see Mark 10:17–31 and Luke 18:18–30. Some take these passages to apply only to men and the priesthood. I disagree with this view. They contain valuable lessons for women considering religious life. This is not to say, however, that religious life is the same as the priesthood. It is not. Nor do I argue that women can or should become priests. See Sara Butler, *The Catholic Priesthood and Women: A Guide to the Teaching of the Church* (Chicago: Hillenbrand, 2007).

the poor, and you will have treasure in heaven; and come, follow me."[28]

When the young man states that he already complies with the commandments, Our Lord asks for more. He invites the young man to climb further the mountain of sanctity and perfection. He asks the young man to do this by committing to a life of poverty and obedience: He invites the young man to enter religious life.

Sadly, many religious are uncomfortable with this teaching. They are reticent to see their celibate life of poverty and obedience as objectively superior in any way. They are afraid to tell my generation and now yours what the Church has always taught: religious life is the more perfect path to take if one desires to be a saint.[29]

Keep in mind that this teaching does not denigrate marriage.[30] I don't doubt that I can become a saint through marriage, and I am extremely grateful to God for the graces He has given to me through the Sacrament of Holy Matrimony.[31] However, it is also true that while marriage is good

---

[28] Emphasis added.

[29] In a beautiful and eloquent essay for *First Things*, writer Patricia Snow observes that while the Church is keen to discard its traditional view of the importance and superiority of religious life, "non-Catholic, equivocally Catholic, or anti-Catholic literature or films" continue to grasp and understand the "Church's traditional ordering of her internal life" and frequently use the character of a priest or nun as a metonym for the Church. Patricia Snow, "Dismantling the Cross," *First Things* (April 2015).

[30] Recognizing that religious life is more efficacious than marriage in preparing one for heaven does not necessarily imply that marriage is poor, bad, or worthless.

[31] Our marriage is a great blessing to me. My husband's love and loyalty to me are a reflection of God's own love and faithfulness, and I have flourished within the loving, protective confines of this relational tabernacle.

and beautiful, spiritually speaking, the religious life is outstanding.

Pope Pius XII addressed this particular problem in the 1954 papal encyclical *Sacra virginitas*, stating that those who challenged "this doctrine of the excellence of virginity and of celibacy and of their superiority over the married state" hurt "the souls of the faithful":

> This doctrine of the excellence of virginity and of celibacy and of their superiority over the married state was, as We have already said, revealed by our Divine Redeemer and by the Apostle of the Gentiles; so too, it was solemnly defined as a dogma of divine faith by the holy council of Trent, and explained in the same way by all the holy Fathers and Doctors of the Church. Finally, We and Our Predecessors have often expounded it and earnestly advocated it whenever occasion offered. But recent attacks on this traditional doctrine of the Church, the danger they constitute, and the harm they do to the souls of the faithful lead Us, in fulfillment of the duties of Our charge, to take up the matter once again in this Encyclical Letter, and to reprove these errors which are so often propounded under a specious appearance of truth.[32]

The Second Vatican Council followed suit. In *Optatam totius*, Pope Paul VI encouraged seminarians "to acknowledge the

---

Second, our "calling" to be adoptive parents is a beautiful gift. God has entrusted our children to us and I am delighted to be the mother of these precious little souls.

[32] Pius XII, *Sacra virginitas* (March 25, 1954), §32.

duties and dignity of Christian matrimony, which is a sign of the love between Christ and the Church," but also instructed them to "recognize . . . the *surpassing excellence* of virginity consecrated to Christ so that with a maturely deliberate and generous choice they may consecrate themselves to the Lord by a complete gift of body and soul."[33]

This doctrine of the Church was again reiterated by Saint John Paul II in the 1996 Apostolic Exhortation, *Vita consecrata*:

> As a way of showing forth the Church's holiness, *it is to be recognized that the consecrated life*, which mirrors Christ's own way of life, *has an objective superiority*. Precisely for this reason, it is an especially rich manifestation of Gospel values and a more complete expression of the Church's purpose, which is the sanctification of humanity. The consecrated life proclaims and in a certain way anticipates the future age, when the fullness of the Kingdom of heaven, already present in its first fruits and in mystery, will be achieved, and when the children of the resurrection will take neither wife nor husband, but will be like the angels of God (cf. Mt 22:30).[34]

A clearer understanding of this passage is possible when we reference the work Saint John Paul II did as Karol Wojtyła in

---

[33] Paul VI, *Optatam totius* (October 28, 1965), §10. Emphasis added. This, of course, does not conflict with the universal call to holiness which was also proclaimed by the Council in *Lumen gentium*. See the chapter of this book titled "A Universal Call to Sanctity."

[34] John Paul II, *Vita consecrata* (March 25, 1996), §32. Emphasis in original text.

his masterpiece, *Love and Responsibility*:

> The value of virginity, and indeed its superiority to
> marriage, which is expressly emphasized in the Bible
> (1 Corinthians 7), and has always been maintained
> in the teaching of the Church, is to be found in the
> exceptionally important part which virginity plays in
> realizing the kingdom of God on earth. The kingdom
> of God on earth is realized in that particular people
> gradually prepare and perfect themselves for eternal
> union with God. In this union the objective develop-
> ment of the human person reaches its highest point.
> Spiritual virginity, the self-giving of a human person
> wedded to God Himself, expressly anticipates this
> eternal union with God and points the way to it.[35]

It is important to note that in *Vita consecrata*, Saint John Paul
II describes the consecrated life as "objectively" superior. This
objectivity relates to the general efficacy of this way of life in
attaining holiness (all things being equal) rather than its suit-
ability for a particular person. Subjectively, a person should
do what God wants her to do. Nevertheless, where there is a
choice—that is, if a person can live the religious life because
she has the aptitude for it and is called—she should choose it
since it provides a better means for achieving sanctity.

Saint Teresa of the Andes understood this basic premise.
As a teenager she wrote to her confessor, Father José Blanche:

---

[35] Karol Wojtyła, *Love and Responsibility* (San Francisco: Ignatius, 1991),
255.

What I want to know, Rev. Father, is where you think I'll become holy more quickly; for, as I've told you on different occasions, Our Lord has made me understand that I would not live a long life. Union with God is the essential thing. Where will I go to be united with God more quickly? I pray a lot that Our Lord will make known to me His divine will, because that's the only thing I'm looking for.[36]

The answer, of course, was religious life, and she entered the enclosed cloister of the Carmel of Los Andes.

Of course, non-Catholics understand this too. In her book, *Three Came Home*, Agnes Newton Keith writes about her experience in a Japanese prisoner-of-war camp during World War II where she was interned for a number of years with a large group of Catholic nuns and religious sisters.[37] "I was thrown in close contact with a community of Roman Catholic nuns," and this was, she says, "the best thing that happened to me in captivity."[38] Prior to this, the non-Catholic Agnes "really knew nothing about them":

Now in Kuching, I met nuns, as women, and sisters, and mothers; hard workers, and my friends. Here I met them as people who sang, and laughed, and made jokes and had fun. As people who prayed and fasted as a privilege and a joy, not as a duty. As women who had chosen a way of life, not had it thrust on them, and

---

[36] Teresa of the Andes to Fr. José Blanche, 13 December 1918, in *Letters*, 87.
[37] See footnote 26 for the distinction between nun and religious sister.
[38] Agnes Newton Keith, *Three Came Home* (Boston, MA: Little, Brown, and Company, 1947), 100.

who loved it. As women who never, never refused to give help. As women who were sorry for *us*, merciful to *us*, and tried to help *us*, because *they* had the Way and the Life; while we, poor fleshly creatures of this world and now cut off from this world, had nothing. We secular women, living with our own sex had already found ourselves, and found ourselves wanting. We could not get on without men, their stimulation, comfort, companionship. . . . But the sisters were different, they were complete. They were wedded to Christ and the Church, and for the first time in my life in Kuching, I saw that this was so. Then for the first time it became credible to me that they were Holy Brides. They formed in general a background of prayer and peace, for the rest of our world which was mad.[39]

Agnes was so impressed with the sisters that she sought to understand what made them so different from the other women in the camp:

All through camp life, I studied the sisters and loved them, and I tried very hard to learn. I learned one thing: . . . We wives had put our minds and our hearts on our husbands, which is what a good marriage is, and we now were without them, and lost. The sisters had put minds and hearts on God only, and they had Him, and they only were whole.[40]

---

[39] Ibid., 100–101. Emphasis in original.
[40] Ibid., 104.

The calling to religious life is a great gift. It isn't given to everyone and those who do receive it should be grateful. If Our Lord asks you to follow Him in ascending the path of perfection, are you ready to say yes or, like the rich young man, will you turn away?

READING LIST

Prayers for Vocations to the Religious Life and the Priesthood

+ Congregation for the Clergy, *Eucharistic Adoration for the Sanctification of Priests and Spiritual Motherhood* (https://www.ewtn.com/library/CURIA/ccladoration.pdf)
+ Website: *Invisible Monastery* (http://www.invisiblemonastery.com/)
+ *The Raccolta*, §604–608[41]

History of Religious Life

+ Richard Butler, O.P., *Religious Vocations: An Unnecessary Mystery*, Chapter II: "How it Happened"
+ Council of Major Superiors of Women Religious, *The Foundations of Religious Life: Revisiting the Vision*, Introduction: "Historical Context"

Overview of Religious Life

+ Cardinal Francis Arinze, *Radical Discipleship: Consecrated Life and the Call to Holiness*

---

[41] *The Roccolta* is a collection of prayers and devotions for which popes have granted indulgences. This edition was first published in 1957 by Benzinger Brothers Inc. and was reprinted in 2010 by Loretto Publishing.

Superiority of Religious Life

+ Patricia Snow, "Dismantling the Cross: A Call for Renewed Emphasis on the Celibate Vocation," *First Things*, April 2015

The Evangelical Counsels

Poverty

+ Thomas Dubay, S.M., *Happy Are You Poor: The Simple Life and Spiritual Freedom*

Celibacy

+ Andrew Apostoli, C.F.R., *When God Asks for an Undivided Heart: Choosing Celibacy in Love and Freedom*
+ Raniero Cantalamessa, O.F.M. Cap., *Virginity: A Positive Approach to Celibacy for the Sake of the Kingdom of Heaven*
+ Thomas Dubay, S.M., *"And You Are Christ's": The Charism of Virginity and the Celibate Life*
+ Benedict J. Groeschel, C.F.R., *The Courage to be Chaste*
+ Karol Wojtyła, *Love and Responsibility*, Chapter 4: "Justice Towards the Creator: Vocation: Mystical and Physical Virginity"

Obedience

+ Reginald Garrigou-Lagrange, O.P., *The Three Ages of the Interior Life: Prelude of Eternal Life*, Volume 2, Part 3, Chapter 15: "The Grandeur of Obedience"

Vocare: "To Call" and "To Name"

Dear Marie Therese,

Your efforts to discern will likely be hindered rather than helped by the general confusion surrounding the word "vocation." Saint Teresa Benedicta of the Cross, better known as Edith Stein, wrote about this problem in 1931:

> In everyday usage, the hackneyed word "vocation" retains little of its original connotation. When young people are about to graduate, one wonders what occupation they should pursue; the question whether women should enter professional life or stay at home has been controversial for some time. Here the term designating vocation does not convey much more than gainful employment. The original meaning of the word survives only in particular allusions, i.e. when one says that a person has missed his vocation or when one speaks of a religious vocation. These idioms signify that a vocation is something to which a person must be *called*.[41]

Even then, "vocation" had become synonymous with "occupation"; a conflation which obscures the true and original meaning of the word. This confusion is the reason we

---

[41] Edith Stein, "The Separate Vocations of Man and Woman According to Nature and Grace" in *The Collected Works of Edith Stein*, vol. 2, *Essays on Woman*, 2nd ed. (Washington, DC: ICS Publications, 1987), 59. Emphasis in original.

sometimes hear people speaking about their professional life in vocational terms. It is also why many young people decide on an occupation, industry, or field of work before considering whether they might be called to the priesthood or religious life.

"Vocation" is derived from the Latin word "vocare," meaning "to call." In Italian, it also means "to name." Saint Edith Stein asked, "Yet, what does it mean to be called?" Her answer was that a "call must have been sent from someone, to someone, *for something* in a *distinct manner*."[42] Vocation, as such, is relational. It is about one's intimate relationship with God and what God intends for us through this relationship.

He is calling us, first and foremost, to be His daughters and sons. He is calling us into a relationship with Him in which He "names" us as His own: "I have called you by name" (Is 43:1). This is the universal call to sanctity.

Second, He calls us further into a familial relationship with Him through which we mirror Him in a particular and irreplaceable way. God invites some women to enter the religious life: He asks them to unite themselves exclusively and entirely to Him. A religious vocation originates when Jesus invites a woman to be His spouse and she agrees to follow Him on the path of perfection by committing to the evangelical counsels. In this she reflects Christ. She becomes a living mirror and icon of the Son (Second Person of the Holy Trinity) in His relationship to the Father (First Person of the Holy Trinity) and in the way that the Son generously sacrificed Himself on earth—on the Cross—out of love for the Father, for all of the Father's children. It is a love that is directed to-

---

[42] Ibid.

wards the One but flows out to affect all.

Others are to be wives and mothers: they become coop-erators with His creative power as mothers and co-workers in His redemptive effort as they work and pray for the salva-tion and well-being of their husbands and children. It is in the specificity of her vocational love that the wife and mother be-comes a living mirror and icon of the Holy Spirit (the Third Person of the Holy Trinity). The Holy Spirit is the love of the Father (the First Person) for the Son (the Second Person) and vice versa: He is the Love of a specific Person for a spe-cific Person. The wife and mother is asked to direct herself towards the One in a love that flows out to affect (primarily) a specific one or few (her husband and any children they have).

Compared with this rich understanding of "vocation," its sense as "occupation" is impoverished and peripheral. What distinguishes the primary sense of vocation (meaning reli-gious life, with marriage being a secondary instance) from the tertiary (by which I mean occupation or paid employment) are the relational and irreplaceable aspects of the former, and the way in which they orientate a person towards eternity.

When one enters into religious life or marriage, a gift is given. That gift is a "person." When I married I was given the gift of my husband. He gave himself to me and I to him. A re-ligious sister is given the gift of a Person too: the gift of Christ Himself as her spouse. He gives Himself to her and she gives herself to Him.

This relational aspect is what makes these "vocations" significant and beautiful. A person is of infinite worth. One's spouse (earthly or heavenly) is irreplaceable. One's children are irreplaceable. And we are irreplaceable too.

When I left my job as an attorney, my work, office, and desk were allocated to another attorney. My work (the tertiary sense of "vocation") was replicable. This is not so as a wife and mother. The person-to-person relationships and interactions between my family members and myself are unique. Even if my role were to be fulfilled by another, the unique, loving relationship between my child and me, or my husband and me, cannot be duplicated.

The emphasis placed in these states of life (i.e., marriage or religious life) on relationships—particularly one's intimate relationship with God—orientates the woman toward eternity. The relationship she enters into with God and then the souls she encounters and loves in His name extend beyond time and place. This distinguishes religious life and marriage from avocational work. I will not take the legal papers I wrote as an attorney with me to heaven, but I do hope to share the beatific vision with my husband and children. Likewise, the religious sister aspires to enter into eternity where she can forever praise and behold her Eternal Spouse.

Saint Edith Stein tells us, "woman's destiny stems from eternity. She must be mindful of eternity to define her vocation in this world. If she complies with her vocation, she achieves her destiny in eternal life."[43]

Because the religious life is a supernatural calling—something above and beyond what we are naturally inclined to—it stands out as a very particular and special calling. Some people fall into marriage by default. They do not enter into the married state with the conscious purpose of serving

---

[43] Edith Stein, "Spirituality of the Christian Woman" in *The Collected Works of Edith Stein*, 118.

and loving God, and they might have a limited conception of sacrifice. It is very difficult to "fall" into religious life—one chooses religious life because she makes a conscious choice in favor of God and heaven. This is the reason people often say, "She has a vocation," meaning that a young woman is called to religious life.

Given the hierarchy of the different senses of the word "vocation," it is appropriate to determine who you are called to be and what you intend to do in a similarly hierarchal manner. When you consider whether you are called to religious life, try to answer these questions in the following order:

1. Do I want to be a saint?
2. If yes, am I called to be a nun or religious sister?
3. If yes, does God want me in a contemplative or semi-active order? Which order should I join?
4. If I am not called to religious life, should I enter into the married state? If yes, with whom?
5. If I am to marry or remain celibate in the world, what occupation or gainful employment should I pursue?

In this hierarchy, the question of occupation comes last, after more pressing questions related to your ultimate happiness and fulfillment are answered first. Ask Saint Edith Stein to aid you in these deliberations. She understands discernment and she will intercede on your behalf to obtain the clarity you need.

Reading List

+ Edith Stein, *The Collected Works of Edith Stein, Volume 2: Essays on Woman*
+ Karol Wojtyła, *Love and Responsibility*, Chapter IV: "Justice Towards the Creator: Vocation"

Stages of Formation: Room for Error

Dear Marie Therese,

The discernment process does not end when you enter the convent but continues as you progress through the various stages of formation. Unlike marriage, which by its nature must be permanent and exclusive from the very start, religious life does not acquire permanency until solemn vows have been professed.

There are a number of stages you must pass through first—all of which are designed to help you and your religious community see whether you really do have a vocation to religious life. This is a process of "dual discernment" whereby you continue to discern whether you have a vocation to religious life and the religious community continues to discern whether you have a vocation with them.

The first stage is the postulancy. You'll have somewhere between four to twenty-four months as a postulant (depending on the order and whether it is semi-active or contemplative). Next you'll enter the novitiate phase. You'll be a novice for another year or two. Following this is the first profession where you'll make temporary vows in which you commit to living as a religious sister for another two to three years. In some orders you'll then renew these temporary vows for another two years. Only after all this do you make a profession of perpetual vows. You will have discerned the religious life for at least six years before making a permanent commitment—often longer.

In *The Song at the Scaffold*, Gertrud von le Fort likens the novitiate to "a question which can be answered in the negative."[44] At some point along the way, you might be told that it is not for you. You might not be accepted by the order of your choice. Conversely, you might realize that this is not where God wants you. You can leave any time during the postulancy or novitiate, which means, of course, that you can *enter* religious life without permanently closing the door to marriage. In religious life, there is room for error that does not exist in marriage.

If you are questioning whether you are called, then prepare for religious life: discern, pray, research, and enter. Entrust the process to God. Say a prayer of obstruction asking God to keep you from entering religious life if this is not His will for you. Then proceed prayerfully and courageously.

READING LIST

+ Pierre de Calan, *Cosmas or the Love of God* (fiction)
+ Gertrud von le Fort, *The Song at the Scaffold* (fiction)
+ Rumer Godden, *In This House of Brede* (fiction)
+ Sister Marie, O.C.D, *A Few Lines to Tell You: My Life in Carmel*

---

[44] Gertrud von le Fort, *The Song at the Scaffold* (San Francisco: Ignatius, 2011), 57.

DISCERNING THAT YOU ARE NOT CALLED TO RELIGIOUS LIFE

Dear Marie Therese,

I know that you are also attracted to marriage and family life. You come from a family where family life is as it should be. Your parents' marriage is a strong, happy, and holy one. You see them experience the great joy that comes with openness to children and a generous and holy disposition towards marriage.

Do not forget, however, that genuine joy is also found in religious life. The joy of a Christian marriage and family is a reflection of the love and joy of the Blessed Trinity. Religious communities (families) share in this same joy. The context in which it is experienced is different, but it is the same joy because it comes from the same source.

It may be that married life is for you. As Mother Saint-Raphaël tells the protagonist in *Mariette in Ecstasy*, "God sometimes wants our desire for a religious vocation but not the deed itself."[45]

If this is the case—especially if this understanding comes after a protracted discernment period—you might wonder why? What was the point? Why, Lord, did you drag me through this process, and for what good? You might feel disappointment, confusion, or a sense of failure.

Those who discover that they do not have a vocation to

---

[45] Ron Hansen, *Mariette in Ecstasy* (New York: Harper Perennial, 1991), 174.

religious life after entering the convent might also experience feelings of humiliation and abandonment.[46]

When Saint Zélie Martin learned she was not called to religious life she wrote: "Lord, since, unlike my sister, I am not worthy to be your bride, I will enter the married state in order to fulfill Your Holy will. I beg of You to give me many children and to let them be consecrated to You."[47] One gets a sense of the sorrow she felt and yet she turned the situation into something very holy: she accepted Our Lord's will and responded generously.

Maria von Trapp (of *The Sound of Music* fame) was devastated when she realized she was to marry rather than enter religious life:

> I knew this was final, and no argument was possible. Yes, it was true, I had wanted to know the Will of God; but now I had met it, I refused to accept it. All my happiness was shattered, and my heart, which so longed to give itself entirely to God, felt rejected. Heavy waves of disappointment and bitterness swept over it. With dry eyes I stared down at the large ring on the Abbess' hand, and mechanically I read over and over again the engraved words around the big amethyst: "God's Will Hath No Why."[48]

---

[46] The same often occurs when a soul discovers that it needs to leave the religious community it entered and find or found another. I recommend those in this position read *A Calling: An Autobiography and the Founding of the Maronite Monks of Adoration* by Abbot William, M.M.A (Leonine Publishers, 2012).

[47] Fr. Stéphane-Joseph Fiat, O.F.M., *The Story of a Family: The Home of St. Therese of Lisieux* (Charlotte, NC: Tan Books, 1948), 33.

[48] Maria Augusta Trapp, *The Story of the Trapp Family Singers* (New York:

If it becomes apparent that you do not have a religious vocation, do not be discouraged. Do not allow yourself to become lax as I did. Still strive to love Our Lord just as much. In one sense, there is now even more merit to your efforts in pursuing unity with God, for these efforts are no longer being done out of an inexperienced or romanticized understanding of religious life, but in humble submission to His will.

Let Our Lord use this as an opportunity to purify your love for Him. How much greater the value of your interior life when continued even though you feel disappointed.

Know that nothing you do in preparing for religious life will be wasted. To lead a holy life in the world and to continue to climb spiritually as a layperson is no easy thing. The insights, graces, and habits developed during your discernment period will help as you enter your lay life. If you allow Him, God will put them to great use elsewhere.

Maria von Trapp used the graces and wisdom she received in her religious training to joyfully raise ten children. Her book, *The Trapp Family Singers*, inspired the musical and subsequent film, *The Sound of Music*—arguably the most widely seen Catholic film of the last century.[49]

In the case of the Martins, God used the graces, habits, and virtues they developed—as well as their understanding of

---

William Morrow, 1949; reprinted 2002), 59.

[49] Maria von Trapp's lesser-known book, *Around the Year with the Trapp Family* (unfortunately now out of print) is, in my opinion, the best guide available for mothers seeking to integrate the liturgy and other faith practices into everyday family life. Other excellent books of this sort (thankfully, still in print) are by Mary Reed Newland (*How to Raise Good Catholic Children* and *The Year & Our Children: Catholic Family Celebrations for Every Season*) and Rev. Francis X. Weiser (*The Holyday Book; The Christmas Book;* and *The Easter Book*).

the spiritual and religious life—to form them as teachers and guardians of their children, all of whom entered religious life. Saints Zélie and Louis were their first teachers and mentored them in the spiritual life. Saints Zélie and Louis would not have been able to do this so well without the training they received at the hands of Our Lord during their own discernment.

Parents train their children. It is unsurprising that the children of talented actors often become actors. It is not just nepotism at work. They tutor their children in their craft—not always deliberately but by exposing them to the habits, discussion, work, and ways of the dramatic arts. A similar thing often happens to the children of lawyers, doctors, tradesmen, academics, etc.

In a similar way, all parents school their children in the spiritual life. They are responsible not only for teaching their children about God but also showing them how to relate to Him and love Him. Parents must witness to their children by providing them a living example of the spiritual life. Parents can't do this well unless they have a loving relationship with Jesus enriched by means of prayer and participation in the sacraments.

If you have been through a period of discernment and discover that God wishes you to marry, ask God, if it is His will, to give you religious souls to raise. Ask Him also for the graces to do this well and with humility.

READING LIST

+ Stephane-Joseph Piat, *The Story of a Family: The Home of St. Thérèse of Lisieux*
+ Maria von Trapp, *The Trapp Family Singers*

A UNIVERSAL CALL TO SANCTITY

Dear Marie Therese,

Do you recall when Anna wanted to know what the difference would be for someone preparing to enter marriage rather than religious life? My answer was "nothing." You all looked so surprised!

What I meant by this is that both states of life require similar preparation insofar as the call to be a saint is universal, and the way we become saints is the same for everyone: seeking union with God by living out His will, with Him, every moment of every day. The means for achieving this are the same regardless of one's state of life, for sanctity cannot be achieved without a rich prayer life, mortification, the sacraments, and a disavowal and avoidance of sin. Detachment, self-denial, and prayer is asked of all, regardless of whether we marry or enter religious life.

Of course, certain aspects of one's preparation will differ according to the state of life one is preparing for. How the universal call to sanctity is lived out on a day-to-day basis varies and, therefore, some of the practical means of preparation will also vary.

An enclosed nun pours herself out in prayer and obedience. She serves Our Lord and His Church through her primary "work" of prayer. One enclosed contemplative I know has adopted my home country as a special apostolate of hers. Although she has never been to Australia, she offers her routine and day of prayer, her obedience and her struggles, joys and suffering at least in part for the Catholic Church and its members in Australia. Hers is an interior service. She is an apostle of prayer. Saint John Paul II described the role of a cloistered nun in this way:

> To leave the world to devote oneself in solitude to deeper and constant prayer is none other than a special way of being an apostle. It would be an error to consider cloistered nuns as creatures separated from their contemporaries, isolated and seemingly cut off from the world and the Church. Rather, they are present to them, and in a deeper way, with the same tenderness as that of Christ.[50]

A sister in a semi-active order also prays, for prayer is the foundation of all she does. In addition to this, however, she is also called to participate in active service.[51] A Sister of Life might run a healing retreat for post-abortive women, or she might spend time praying with a brave young woman discerning whether to place her unborn baby for adoption. A Franciscan Sister of the Renewal (colloquially known as the CFR Sisters) might spend part of her day running a soup kitchen or teaching catechesis to children at a parish in a poor neighborhood. A Dominican Sister (such as the Dominican Sisters of Saint Cecilia in Nashville, Tennessee, or the Dominican Sisters of Mary, Mother of the Eucharist in Ann Arbor, MI) might also be a kindergarten or high school teacher.

---

[50] John Paul II, *The Meaning of Vocation* (New York: Scepter Press, 1998), 31–32.

[51] Typically corporal or spiritual works of mercy.

Similarly, a woman who marries should pour herself out in prayer and service. Like a semi-active religious sister, the life of a married woman must be rooted in prayer and service, but the form of her service is somewhat narrower and more focused than that of a religious sister. A sister might serve the people in one community and then, when transferred to a different convent of the same order, will work with another group of people in a different area with different needs. In contrast, the primary recipients of a mother's service are unchanging. The service of a wife and mother must be constantly directed towards the good of her spouse and any children given to the marriage. It is to the good of these specific souls that she must tend.

As put by Saint Claude de la Colombière, the mother's field and vineyard is her family:

> What are you doing at home if you do not busy yourselves in the upbringing of your children? It is the only thing you have to do. It is in this that God wishes you to serve Him. It is for this that He has established Christian marriage. It is of this that He will demand an account of you. You have amassed property for them. Is this what God expects of you? "Come now," He will say to you on the Day of Judgment, "give me an account of that soul that I have confided to you. What has become of it? That was your field, the vineyard which the Lord had given to you to cultivate. To what degree of holiness have you led them? With what principles have you inspired them? Are they good? Do they fear God? Are they instructed in

our mysteries?" Some will have no answer to make for they will not know what to make of those questions.[52]

A woman who knows she will likely enter the married state would do well to learn how to cook, sew, and understand the basics of keeping a home.[53] Such things might seem lowly or unimportant but they are part of a wide array of skills a mother can draw on in building a home and life for her loved ones. Willa Cather's young Canadienne, Cécile Auclair, in *Shadows on the Rocks*, articulates this well when, observing the kitchen of her Québec home, she notes:

> These coppers, big and little, these brooms and clouts and brushes, were tools; and with them one made, not shoes or cabinet-work, but life itself. One made a climate within a climate; one made the days, the complexion, the special flavour, the special happiness of each day as it passed; one made life.[54]

A woman desiring marriage should also learn how to budget, and will benefit from reading many of the wonderful books

---

[52] Georges Guitton, S.J., *Perfect Friend* (New York: Herder, 1956), 65–66. Quoted in Mary Reed Newland, *The Saints and Our Children: Lives of the Saints and the Catholic Lessons to be Learned from Them* (Charlotte, NC: TAN Books, 1958).

[53] This might seem like antiquated advice but I think it helpful for the modern young woman to hear. When I married, I had several degrees but I didn't clean house and I had no idea how to cook, do laundry, or fold clothes. I certainly had never heard of meal planning. When I left practice as an attorney and took on the bulk of our domestic obligations, I regretted not being more proficient.

[54] Willa Cather, *Shadows on the Rock* (London: Vintage Classics, 1995), 159–160.

written to help couples prepare for marriage (see below for a reading list). If she didn't grow up in a big family with younger siblings, she might want to babysit or spend time with families with young children. Motherhood can come as a shock to those without some experience caring for young children!

However, like a woman preparing to enter religious life, a young woman preparing herself for marriage should also strive to attend daily Mass and weekly Confession. She too should commit to a schedule of spiritual reading and daily prayer. Likewise, she should get to know her faith by reading Scripture, the Catholic Catechism, and so on. She might decide, however, that—absent a particular inclination to do so—she will not recite the Divine Office.

Whether as a religious or as a wife or mother, we can be assured that the gift of ourselves—a "pouring out," as I have described it—will make us more authentically ourselves. It is how we become the person God calls us to be. In the words of Saint John Paul II (then Karol Wojtyła) in *Love and Responsibility*:

> A person who has a vocation must not only love someone but be prepared to give himself or herself for love. We have said already in our analysis of love that this self-giving may have a very creative effect on the person: the person fulfills itself most effectively when it gives itself most fully.[55]

---

[55] Karol Wojtyła, *Love and Responsibility*, 256–257.

Reading List

Spiritual Preparation for Marriage

- Javier Abad and Eugenio Fenoy, *Marriage: A Path to Sanctity*
- Dietrich von Hildebrand, *Marriage: The Mystery of Faithful Love*
- Fulton J. Sheen, *Three to Get Married*
- Karol Wojtyła, *Love and Responsibility*
- Scott Hahn, *The First Society: The Sacrament of Matrimony and the Restoration of the Social Order*

SPIRITUAL MOTHERHOOD

Dear Marie Therese,

Sometimes people think that they can discern whether something is God's will by the amount of repugnance they feel towards it. They assume that it must be God's will if it is taxing and without appeal. It's become a shorthand way of saying that we ought to be generous.

This has not been my experience. To paraphrase Saint Thomas Aquinas: grace builds on and perfects nature.[56] God will not call us to something that is not a fitting good for us. One's vocation is a tremendous gift from God and it is not in God's nature to create and gift something to us that isn't also supremely good for us. This is not to say that we won't have to do or suffer through things that are difficult or arduous, but rather—especially in the case of a vocation—He isn't going to invite us into something that we're particularly ill-suited to.[57]

Not all women desire earthly marriage or family life. Some of these women are indeed called to religious life. A muted desire for marriage and motherhood can be a sign that a woman is called to give her heart and life to the Eternal Spouse. Saint Teresa of the Andes had no desire for earthly marriage:

---

[56] *ST* I-I, q. 1, a. 8: "Since therefore grace does not destroy nature but perfects it, natural reason should minister to faith as the natural bent of the will ministers to charity."

[57] There is, however, sometimes a misalignment between what we think we'd like to do and who we think we are, and who we actually are and what we really do need in order to flourish. A woman might think she wants to marry but is called to religious life. And another—such as myself—might desire religious life but is better suited (in capacity and need) to marriage.

Well, how can one fall in love with an imperfect being, with someone in whom one observes deficiencies
of character and gifts each day, as well as a host of de-
fects? How can we love someone when God set limits
for us in this love? Above all other beings, we should
love and serve the Creator. Only then do human
beings become the second expression of love. No, I
cannot understand that kind of love; I don't understand how people can love that way.[58]

A woman is wrong, however, if she thinks her disincli-
nation for marriage or children means that she doesn't need
or can't provide familial love, spousal love, or spiritual motherhood. Every woman has the capacity for motherhood and
family life (even if she doesn't understand, perceive, or actu-
alize it). As a religious, she'll be a spiritual mother and she'll
have a robust, wonderful, and sometimes demanding family
life with her religious sisters. She will also be married and she
will have a spouse—her Eternal Spouse, Jesus Christ.

For a beautiful cinematic portrayal of spiritual motherhood in religious life, I suggest watching the 2014 French
film, *Marie's Story*. I also recommend reading Rumer Godden's *In This House of Brede*. The protagonist, Dame Philippa,
leaves a very successful and high-powered position in the
secular world to become a contemplative nun. Dame Philippa was once married and lost her husband and son in tragic
circumstances. She understands the sorrow of the world and
longs for the eternal. As a Benedictine nun, she resists spiritual motherhood. She doesn't want it and certainly not on the

---

[58] Teresa of the Andes to Elena Salas Gonzalez, *Letters*, 70–71.

terms set out by God. By being open to God's grace, however, she starts to imitate Mary—accepting that she can't replace her son but that she can embrace and appreciate spiritual motherhood nonetheless. Our Lord responds by extending His mercy to her and she experiences transformative healing, forgiveness, and peace through her spiritual motherhood.

Sister Cecily, on the other hand, is younger than Dame Philippa and enters the convent of Brede a virginal young woman with no desire for anything but religious life. Sister Cecily seems so perfect for religious life that the other sisters doubt the authenticity of her vocation. Her story arc illustrates the capacity for marriage even in a religious who seemingly lacks any desire for earthly marriage. Over time Sister Cecily comes to understand the sacrifice she has made and longs for children. When she is given the opportunity to leave the convent, marry her former fiancé, and have a family, she realizes and accepts that she is already married to Christ and that this supernatural marriage is worth more to her than even physical motherhood.

Both of these characters found that God was generous and surprising in His loving gift of Himself. This was also the case for Saint Teresa of the Andes:

> Believe me. I'm speaking to you sincerely: I used to believe it was impossible ever to fall in love with a God who is unseen; with someone who can't be hugged and touched. But today I can affirm with my hand over my heart that God completely makes up for that sacrifice, You feel that love so much and those caresses from Our Lord, that it seems God is there by your side. I

feel Him so intimately united to me, that I want nothing more, except the beatific vision in heaven. I feel I'm filled with God, and then I hold Him close to my heart and ask Him to make me experience the perfections of His love. There's no separation between us. Where I go, God is with me in my poor heart. That's the little house where I dwell; it's my heaven here on earth. I live with God; and, despite being on walks, we converse with each other without anyone being able to surprise us or interrupt us. If you knew Him enough, you'd love Him. If you were with Him for one hour, you'd know just what heaven on earth is.[59]

Saint Teresa of the Andes is not describing spiritual dryness but the springtime that comes after a spiritual winter. She has been given spiritual union with God—the Divine Intimacy.

Surely, you might think, "That is not possible for me! I am too ordinary." But yes! Yes, it is possible! It is for this that you were made. You are invited to Divine Intimacy with a perfect spouse—perhaps it will not be to the same degree as Saint Teresa of the Andes, and perhaps you'll not experience it quite the same way—but you are called through your vocation to the most sublime and beautiful intimacy with God if you are open and willing to receive it.

There is nothing more beautiful—nothing more sublime—than to be united with love Himself. As Saint Teresa of the Andes asks:

Tell me, is there anything greater on earth than the

---

[59] Ibid.

eternal, immutable, all-powerful God searching out a soul on earth to make her His bride and seeking a human heart to join His own Divine Heart, and in love, achieving the most complete fusion? . . . Think of the greatest love on earth, and what is it in comparison with the love of an Infinite God?[60]

This beautiful, supernatural union is the source of a woman's spiritual motherhood. When a religious enters into her vocation and allows Christ into her heart, He is able to love and serve through her in a very beautiful and particular way. Like a mother, her prayers, sacrifices, and acts of service nourish and sustain His Church. Her love becomes a Eucharistic love with which He feeds His children.

A religious sister or nun is invited into union with Christ not only for her own benefit but for the benefit and good of the entire Church. His children are beneficiaries of her vocation and the entire Church suffers when a woman rejects or ignores God's call to religious life. His children need her motherly love and are poorer for want of her vocation.

READING LIST

+ Congregation for the Clergy, *Eucharistic Adoration for the Sanctification of Priests and Spiritual Motherhood* (https://www.ewtn.com/library/CURIA/ccladoration.pdf)
+ Rumer Godden, *In This House of Brede* (fiction)
+ *Marie's Story* (2014 French film)

---

[60] Ibid.

Part II:
Preparation

Spiritual Direction

Dear Marie Therese,

When we first spoke of your desire to enter religious life, I told you how important it is to find a good confessor and spiritual director. Saint Faustina wrote that she feared for souls that labored without a spiritual director:

> And now when I hear people sometimes say that they have no confessor; that is to say a director, fear takes hold of me, because I know very well how much harm I myself experienced when I did not have this help. It is so easy to go astray when one has no guide![61]

Sometimes Jesus will direct a soul Himself without any intermediary, as was the case with Saint Faustina, but this is the exception and not the rule.[62] Generally Jesus will direct a soul through the intermediary of a priestly spiritual director. Jesus remains the true director of every soul, but asks us to use the means He has provided. He has given us the Sacrament of Confession for this end. In Confession we reveal our souls in such an intimate way that it is possible for Jesus (through His priest) to give us spiritual direction *par excellence*.

In some Catholic movements it has become popular to have a layperson act as one's spiritual director. This is not found much in Catholic tradition, but I pass no judgment on

---

[61] Saint Maria Faustina Kowalska, *Diary*, no. 16.
[62] Ibid., no. 108.

this practice for the laity. However, anyone discerning religious life should have a priest as a spiritual director. Only a priest has the grace of state and stands in for Christ in a special way.[63]

Find a good and holy priest to hear your confessions—preferably on a weekly basis—and to direct you in the spiritual life. The priest should be humble and faithful. Look for a priest with self-restraint. It is beneficial for him to have had some experience directing souls either living the religious life or preparing for entry into religious life. Both Saint Teresa of Ávila and Saint Francis de Sales list prudence as being a particularly important trait in a director. Avoid directors who are rash or impulsive.[64]

The direction of a competent confessor can facilitate great progress in the spiritual life. He will help you avoid mistakes, see faults that need correcting, and hold you back from excess[65] and scruples.[66]

Under the direction of Saint Francis de Sales, Saint Jane

---

[63] This is not to say, however, that you shouldn't also seek out the advice and guidance of a religious sister as you discern.

[64] Saint Teresa of Ávila, *The Life of Saint Teresa of Avila by Herself* (London: Penguin Classics; Reprint edition, 1988), chap. XIII, nos. 24–29.

[65] The restraint cautioned by a director can be as important as the encouragement he gives.

[66] A scruple is an "unfounded apprehension and consequently unwarranted fear that something is a sin which, as a matter of fact, is not. It is not considered here so much as an isolated act, but rather as an habitual state of mind known to directors of souls as a 'scrupulous conscience.' St. Alphonsus describes it as a condition in which one influenced by trifling reasons, and without any solid foundation, is often afraid that sin lies where it really does not.... The judgment is seriously warped, the moral power tired out in futile combat, and then not unfrequently the scrupulous person makes shipwreck of salvation either on the Scylla of despair or the Charybdis of unheeding indulgence in vice." Joseph Delany, "Scruple," *Catholic Encyclopedia* (New York: Appleton, 1912).

Frances de Chantal became a saint. We are told that she "was by nature strong, firm and forceful, but there was a certain hardness and rigidity in her character which was only removed by long years of prayer, suffering and *patient guidance*."[67] Before Saint Jane Frances entered religious life, Saint Francis de Sales "strictly limited her bodily mortifications" and regulated her devotions, reminding her that "she was still a woman in the world, an old man's daughter, and, above all, a mother."[68] Under his directions she grew in holiness, became sweet and mild, and conformed "herself to what she owed to the world whilst she lived in the houses of her father and father-in-law."[69] When it was time for Saint Frances de Chantal to enter religious life, she and Saint Francis de Sales founded the Order of the Visitation of the Virgin Mary.

Just as Saint Francis de Sales did for Saint Jane Frances, a good confessor will help you discern whether you have a calling or not. Often—as was the case for me—your confessor will see before you do whether or not you have a religious vocation.

When you do find a competent spiritual director, read the advice contained in Saint Francis de Sales' superb treatise, *Introduction to the Devout Life*.[70] Saint Francis advises us to be candid and sincere in how we speak to our director:

---

[67] "Jane Frances de Chantal," in *Butler's Lives of the Saints*, ed. Herbert J. Thurston, S.J., and Donald Attwater, vol. 3, *July, August, September* (Notre Dame, IN: Ave Maria Press, 1956), 370. Emphasis added.

[68] Ibid.

[69] Ibid.

[70] *Introduction to the Devout Life* (Totowa, NJ: The Catholic Book Publishing Company, 1946). See pt. I, chap. 4: "The Pursuit of the Devout Life Requires a Guide," and pt. II, chap. 19: "Of Holy Confession."

Let him know the good and the bad that you are in, without lying or dissimulation. In acting thus, the good in you will be assessed and confirmed, and the bad will be corrected and remedied. Your pains will be alleviated and your joys moderated.[71]

Finally, a word of caution: do not engage in "priest shopping." Once you find a confessor, try to be loyal to him. You should not abandon or reject a competent confessor simply because he fails to tell you what you want to hear.

Do not fret. Be at peace and entrust this need to Jesus.

READING LIST

+ Teresa of Ávila, *The Life of Saint Teresa of Ávila by Herself*, Chapter XIII
+ Brett A. Brannen, *To Save a Thousand Souls*, Chapter 7: "The Importance of a Spiritual Director"
+ Francis de Sales, *Introduction to the Devout Life*, Part I, Chapter 4: "The Pursuit of the Devout Life Requires a Guide," and Part II, Chapter 19: "Of Holy Confession"
+ Reginald Garrigou-Lagrange, O.P., *The Three Ages of the Interior Life: Prelude of Eternal Life*, Volume 1, Part 1, Chapter 17: "Spiritual Direction"

---

[71] Ibid, pt I, chap. 4.

The Spiritual Life

Dear Marie Therese,

I have spoken much of the "spiritual life" but have not yet defined or clarified what I mean by this.

The spiritual life is your soul's intimacy with Jesus. It is your growth in and towards God. It is the action of His grace in your soul and it is the progress made by your soul as Christ brings you into an intimate union with Him. It cannot be had without prayer and the sacraments.

Prayer is the work of the spiritual life. Saint Thérèse of Lisieux tells us that "prayer is an aspiration of the heart, it is a simple glance directed to heaven, it is a cry of gratitude and love in the midst of trial as well as joy; finally it is something great, supernatural, which expands my soul and unites me to Jesus."[72]

Saint Alphonsus de Liguori says something similar:

> Meditation is nothing more than a conversation between the soul and God; the soul pours forth to him its affections, its desires, its fears, its requests, and God speaks to the heart, causing it to know his goodness, and the love which he bears it, and what it must do to please him.[73]

---

[72] St. Thérèse of Lisieux, *Story of a Soul*, trans. John Clarke, O.C.D. (Washington, DC: ICS Publications, 1976), 242–243.

[73] St. Alphonsus de Liguori, *Prayer: The Great Means of Salvation and of Perfection* (Potosi, WI: St. Athanasius, 2014). See pt. I, chap. III: "The Ends of Mental Prayer."

The terms "prayer" and "spiritual life" refer to subtly different things but they are inclusive of one another and mutually dependent. Where you are in your spiritual life will impact your prayer. Correspondingly, one is dependent upon prayer to maintain and advance in one's spiritual union with God.

As a religious, the spiritual life will be your true "work." This is true of those called to the semi-active life as well as those who enter a contemplative order. Your life of prayer and your sacramental life should be the foundation of all you do. As a religious, all your other work should flow from and be strengthened by this primary "work."

This also applies to the laity. Right now you are in the lay world living a lay pre-vocation. Now is the time for you to develop your spiritual life. Make prayer, receiving the sacraments, and a life of mortification your primary "work" from which all your other activities flow.

As a single woman in good physical health and of sound mind, you have no impediment to your preparing for religious life in this way. In fact, your entry into this way of life will assist you and your director in determining whether you are called to religious life.

Some notes of caution:

+ A good confessor and spiritual director is essential to growth in the spiritual life. An inexperienced priest who encounters a soul preparing for religious life in this way and sees this soul starting to make progress in the spiritual life—especially when that soul moves past the first stages—may mistake this piety and grace for a vocational calling. He may assume such grace automatically means that the soul is called to religious life. Often this is the case—the soul called to religious life will take flight when preparing this way—but there are exceptions (Saint Louis Martin, Saint Gemma Galgani, and Servant of God Elisabeth Leseur come to mind).

+ Make sure you fulfill the primary duties associated with your life. Right now you are a college student. It would be wrong, for example, to allot so much time to adoration that you fail to assist your family as needed, attend class, or complete your assignments well or on time. Again, this is where having direction from a competent confessor is important.

+ You are in the unusual position of being at home for college. You are also in the unusual position of having parents who support you in your preparation for religious life. Try to arrange your prayer and liturgical life so that it does not disturb or overly burden your parents.

Saint Teresa of Ávila writes much on the stages of prayer and the spiritual life. Read her autobiography, *The Life of Saint Teresa of Ávila by Herself*. This will help you understand the different types of prayer—the path of prayer through which God will lead you—as well as the various stages of the spiritual life.

I can provide a rough summary of some things you can expect.

Be prepared at the beginning for two things: First, that prayer may sometimes feel like hard work. You may find at the start—and recurring throughout other stages of the spiritual life—that you will do a lot of the talking. Remember the importance of silence and quiet listening in prayer. Do not be discouraged if God is more silent than you'd like Him to be. Empty your heart to Him. Let Him speak to you by reading His Word in Scripture, especially the New Testament and the Psalms.

Establish fixed times for prayer and a daily routine. Stick to this routine. It will seem like a lot of work but God hears you and your effort pleases Him. Slowly and surely—if done with an earnest and humble spirit—you will make progress. Ask God for the grace of perseverance when you experience prayer as difficult or tiresome.

Second, at the start, you may well be granted many sweet consolations. These are like the little treats I give to the children from time to time to encourage good behavior and to show my love and affection for them. In these moments, you will feel great joy and lightness. To begin with, these consolations will be emotional in nature or consist of an intellectual light. That is, they usually invoke the emotions or intellect. These consolations are unmerited gifts from God, given as a sign of love and encouragement as He sees fit. Be careful not to seek them out. Don't try to force God to give these to you, or expect them from Him. They cannot be earned. They are little treats for which you should be thankful. Ask for a spirit of gratitude in accepting these gifts.

Moving forward, you may also experience periods of dryness and darkness. These stages are meant to purify you. There is only so much we can do to purify ourselves. Only God Himself can perfect our souls and He does so—in part—by allowing darkness and dryness into our spiritual life and our work of prayer.

Early on it might be limited to the absence of emotional consolations. There will be no sweetness offered by God and your prayer will feel like hard work. When this occurs, practice mental prayer as before, and continue with your regular prayer routine. This period does not last forever, but it helps strengthen you. This is one way Our Lord corrects your motives. You begin to pray and lead a sacramental life not because of what you get out of it but for love of God. It is a first step in eradicating self-love from your relationship with God.

Darkness can also be intellectual. This will often manifest itself as doubts. You will sit in Mass and although you do believe—for if you attempted to renounce God and the Faith you would struggle to do so—you are plagued by doubts of the intellect. Is the Blessed Sacrament really God? Does God really exist? Will I disappear into nothing when I die? Do I have a soul? Does heaven really exist? And so on. Do not be afraid if this happens. It does not mean that you have lost your faith or fallen from a state of grace. The soul experiencing this type of trial knows God, but for a time God hides Himself from the intellect.

Sometimes the soul can also feel abandoned by God. In such cases, the soul no longer has any sense of God being present or supporting it. The soul feels alone and very far from God. The reality, however, is that while the soul does not perceive God, it is in fact very close to God—or rather God is very close to the soul. God is drawing the soul near to Him while remaining hidden from it.[74]

The soul in this state is being asked to share in the aban-

---

[74] Only in retrospect is one usually able to see what God was doing and how God was supporting the soul at the time.

donment felt by Christ first in the garden of Gethsemane and then on the Cross. Such times are given to purify the soul or as a suffering for the atonement of one's sins and conversion of others.

These trials might occur for very short periods of time, interspersed with consolations and quiet contemplation. For some it may last for weeks, months, or even years at a time. Ask God for perseverance during these times. A good spiritual director is vital.

There is one more facet of prayer to discuss with you—composure and distraction.

Early on, the intellect and imagination can be very active when one tries to pray. Sometimes their activity makes it hard to remain focused on God.

It is somewhat similar to when you must interrupt a task to run after our toddler and preschooler when they are misbehaving. The mere effort to get them to behave and quiet down makes you lose focus on whatever it was that you were initially working on or attempting to do.

Later on this problem can subside and the soul is quiet—it experiences an interior peace and calm. Here God holds the will, intellect, emotions, and imagination. The soul is in and with God, and the emotions, intellect, and imagination are still. They do not fight God's embrace but happily cease their busy activity for a period to behold Him. The soul is calmly aware of God and rests in Him.

It sometimes takes a great act of will to leave this state of prayer. The soul wants to stay this way forever with God. To move out of this state requires effort. This type of prayer is a gift from God and the soul does not want to let go of it.

Following this are further stages of spiritual union. I have insufficient experience and understanding to say anything of use on the topic. Read the *Interior Castle* by Saint Teresa of Ávila and *Greater Perfection: A Means of Achieving Union with God Through Prayer* by Blessed Miriam Teresa Demjanovich. *Greater Perfection* is a little-known masterpiece, written by Blessed Miriam Teresa when she was just a novice.[75] The treatise *Heaven in Faith* by Saint Elizabeth of the Trinity is also insightful, as is Part 4 of Reginald Garrigou-Lagrange's *The Three Ages of the Interior Life*.

Some words of caution: No visions, locutions, or periods of darkness should be sought out or desired by you. God gives them to the soul when and as He sees fit. To seek them out or request them puts the soul in peril. Do not presume that you can handle any of these things. You should also be aware that spiritual experiences can also come from hell, and it isn't always easy to discern the difference.

As you progress in the spiritual life, be careful not to slide back or fall. The higher one climbs, the further one has to fall! Do not let this happen to you. Pray to Our Lady for protection!

---

[75] Blessed Miriam Teresa was asked by her confessor in June 1926 to write a series of conferences for her fellow novice sisters. Her authorship was kept anonymous and revealed to her community only after her death. She died in May 1927—a mere 11 months after she started writing. She had originally hoped to enter Carmel but became a Sister of Charity when she saw that it was God's will for her to be an apostle of sorts to the Sisters of Charity: "to teach them that Martha draws all her strength from Mary" (Mary Zita Geis, *Sister Miriam Teresa Demjanovich* [Convent Station, NJ: Sister Miriam Teresa League of Prayer, 1979], 76). Both *Greater Perfection* and the quoted biography by Sister Mary Zita are available for purchase from the Sisters of Charity of St. Elizabeth in Convent Station, New Jersey.

Reading List

+ Saint Teresa of Ávila, *Life*
+ Saint Teresa of Ávila, *Interior Castle*
+ Blessed Miriam Teresa Demjanovich, *Greater Perfection: A Means of Achieving Union with God Through Prayer* (available for purchase from the Sisters of Charity of Saint Elizabeth in Convent Station, New Jersey)
+ Saint Elizabeth of the Trinity, *The Complete Works, Volume One: Major Spiritual Writings*
+ Gabriel of Saint Mary Magdalen, O.C.D., *Divine Intimacy*
+ *Handbook of Prayers*, Scepter Press
+ Reginald Garrigou-Lagrange, O.P., *The Three Ages of the Interior Life: Prelude of Eternal Life*
+ Saint John of the Cross, *Dark Night of the Soul*
+ Thomas à Kempis, *Imitation of Christ*
+ Jean-Baptiste Chautard, O.C.S.O, *The Soul of the Apostolate*
+ Saint Alphonsus de Liguori, *Prayer: The Great Means of Salvation and of Perfection*
+ Jacques Philippe, *Time for God*
+ Adolphe Tanquerey, *The Spiritual Life: A Treatise on Ascetical and Mystical Theology*

The Mechanics

Dear Marie Therese,

This work of prayer and the mechanics of the spiritual life can be divided into the following areas:

+ prayer,
+ participation in the sacraments,
+ adoration,
+ silence,
+ mortification,
+ annual retreat,
+ fulfillment of duties of state of life,
+ obedience,
+ study,
+ and service.

Prayer

Think of prayer as a practice, not a chore or something to get done. Like practicing a sport, skill, or musical instrument, the practice of prayer builds on itself and becomes easier over time. As with any practice, you should have a regular plan for your prayer life.

The idea is to bookend your day with morning and evening prayer, and intersperse other prayers throughout your day so that it becomes a continuous period of prayer, sacrifice, and adoration. The set periods of prayer allow your heart to remain with God as you do your lay work so that this work is transformed into physical prayer offered to God.

There is a delightful children's book by Claire Branden-burg titled *The Monk Who Grew Prayer* which beautifully illustrates this idea. Although intended primarily for children, it provides adults with a lovely insight into the work, prayers, and ebb and flow of religious life. It is the best introduction to this idea of transformative physical prayer in our day to day lives that I have come across yet.

The schedule I suggest is to be worked up to gradually and practiced only under the supervision of your spiritual direc-tor. It is better to start slowly and to steadily build a cathedral upon a solid and secure foundation than to quickly erect a tall but vulnerable tower made of flimsy materials. Eventually, your schedule might look something like this:

+ *Start*: wake up at a set time every morning. When you hear the alarm, begin your day by reminding yourself what it is for: *For the glory of God and my eternal salvation!*
+ *Morning Exercises*: Read the chapter on Morning Exer-cises in *Introduction to the Devout Life* by Saint Francis de Sales. Start with acts of faith, hope, and love. This might include kneeling and saying something as simple as: *Je-sus, I believe in you. Jesus, I hope in you. Jesus, I love you.*

  Thank God for having preserved you through the night. Include here your daily offering and special intentions. Ask for the graces you need to overcome known and unknown faults. You might then recite three Hail Mary prayers for purity and the Saint Mi-chael prayer for protection.
+ *Morning Prayer*: Give additional time (fifteen to thirty

minutes) to more substantial prayer each morning. You might choose to do this directly after your morning exercises. For you this might mean saying the Divine Office (the Psalter of the Liturgy of the Hours), which will take you through the psalms and prepare you well for religious life (all religious must partake in the Divine Office). Others might choose to read a section from the Bible and meditate on it. Allow your director to guide you as to how much time you allot to this. At the beginning it might be as little as five minutes. Remember, cathedrals are built slowly!

+ *Daily Mass*: If you are able, make it a priority to attend daily Mass. Ask God at Mass for the understanding and graces you need to grow in holiness. Remember to spend time in prayer after Mass to thank God for the sacrifice of the Mass.

+ *Angelus*: Discretely stop at noon, if you can, to say the Angelus.

+ *Study*: Assign perhaps ten to fifteen minutes each day to study. You might choose to read the New Testament or a spiritual book. Ask your confessor for guidance.

+ *Rosary and Divine Mercy Chaplet*: Try to say the rosary and chaplet every day. I used to do this on my bus rides to and from university. Now I do it on my afternoon walk with the children. Do not, however, be tempted to substitute the Chaplet for the Rosary when busy. The latter carries a plenary indulgence if prayed in a church or with others.[76]

---

[76] Note that "to be capable of gaining indulgences, a person must be baptized, not excommunicated, and in the state of grace at least at the end

+ *Blessed Sacrament Visit*: Do you have the opportunity to duck into a church to adore Our Lord in the tabernacle for a minute or two each day?

+ *Evening Prayer*: you should allot another fifteen to thirty minutes to substantial evening prayer. You might wish to say the evening prayers of the Divine Office or incorporate some spiritual reading and reflection into your routine here. Allow your director to guide you as to how much time you should devote to this.

+ *Evening Exercises*: Before you go to bed make an act of faith, hope, and love. Examine your conscience. I quite like the examination found in *Handbook of Prayers* by Scepter Press/Midwest Theological Forum. Recite the Act of Contrition[77] and pray for protection throughout the night. Refer to the section on Evening Exercises in *Introduction to the Devout Life* for further instruction.

This is called a *Plan of Life*. It is sometimes also known as a *Rule of Life*. There is no formula for how to pray or how to plan your daily prayer routine.[78] What I have listed here

---

of the prescribed works. To gain indulgences, however, a capable subject must have at least the general intention of acquiring them and must fulfill the enjoined works in the established time and the proper method, according to the tenor of the grant" (Code of Canon Law, c. 996 §1). See International Commission on English in the Liturgy, *The Handbook of Indulgences* (Totowa, NJ: Catholic Book Publishing, 1992), no. 48.

[77] Act of Contrition: *Oh my God, I am heartily sorry for having offended You, and I detest all my sins, because I dread the loss of heaven and the pains of hell; but most of all because they offend You, my God, who are all good and deserving of my love. I firmly resolve, with the help of Your grace, to sin no more and avoid all occasions of sin.* See also *Handbook of Prayers* (Princeton/Chicago: Scepter Press/Midwest Theological Forum, 2005), 62.

[78] For other examples see Elisabeth Leseur's "Plan of Life" in *The Secret Diary of Elisabeth Leseur: The Woman Whose Goodness Changed her Husband*

are suggestions. Please do not think that the path to sanctity consists in fulfilling a list of activities. Rather, what I want to impart to you is this: the key is to have some sort of prayer routine (with time allotted to mental prayer) that you are faithful to in order to develop and practice fidelity to God, so that—in turn—God can teach your soul how to be with and remain in Him.

Participation in the Sacraments

Regular Confession and Mass will provide you with many graces. They will help you move beyond voluntary venial sins and start to do battle with your more insidious faults.

In addition to attending Sunday Mass you should also strive to attend daily Mass.[79] Start by attending weekday Mass two or three times a week and build up from there. Strive to make a weekly confession of your sins. Your routine of prayer and the sacraments—with perseverance—will turn from a chore to a great joy and pleasure. You will want to be intimate with our Blessed Lord through these means even in times of great spiritual dryness.

---

from Atheist to Priest (Manchester, NH: Sophia Institute, 2002), 68–74. The "Rule of Life" adopted by Saint Teresa of the Andes prior to her entry into religious life can be found in letters no. 30, 35 (duties of state), 36 (prayer, spiritual union, and spiritual reading), and 45 (prayer, duties of state and sacrifice), published in *Letters of Saint Teresa of the Andes*. A more concise summary of Teresa's "Rule of Life" is provided by Jennifer Moorcroft in *God is All Joy*, 69–70.

[79] St. Leonard of Port Maurice, *The Hidden Treasure: Holy Mass* (Charlotte, NC: Tan Books, 2012).

Adoration

Adoration provides us with a foretaste of heaven. When we kneel down before Jesus exposed in the monstrance we join the heavenly court in adoring, worshiping, and praising our King. Adoration of the Blessed Sacrament is a special privilege given to Catholics and we ought to appreciate its divine sublimity.

If you can, allocate thirty to sixty minutes once a week to adoration of the Blessed Sacrament exposed in a monstrance. Many churches have First Friday devotions to the Sacred Heart during which a Holy Hour of meditation and prayer is provided in conjunction with exposition of the Blessed Sacrament. Perhaps you can find a parish nearby which offers this? I find adoration on Friday nights to be a very beautiful way of ending my workweek and beginning the weekend.

Silence

When God called Samuel, he was asleep. All was quiet. Samuel was in a state of quiet repose. There was no background noise. No needless chatter. After seeking counsel from Eli (his spiritual director) on what to do, Samuel finally answers—surrounded by silence—"Lord, I am listening" (see 1 Sam 3).

Aspire to be like Samuel. Surround yourself as much as possible with silence and stillness as Samuel did.

We cannot be ready; we cannot answer that we are listening for the Lord without silence. In the words of Saint Josemaría Escrivá, "silence is the doorkeeper of the interior life."[80]

What do I mean by silence? A stillness and receptiveness that is both internal and external.

---

[80] Saint Josemaría Escrivá, *The Way* (New York: Scepter, 1992), no. 281.

The external imposition of silence is easier than the internal and, in fact, aids it, so I will deal with that first.

Try as much as you can to keep noise around you to a minimum. When you are in the car, for example, choose classical or sacred music over pop music. If you are already sufficiently detached from pop music or the need to listen to music, then opt for no radio or music while driving. Use the silence of the drive to internally converse with God or sit with Him in quiet repose.

Allow yourself only specific times of the day or week to listen to music—preferably classical or sacred. Popular music excites the passions and emotions. It will not help you grow in the spiritual life.

The same goes for television and movies. Over time you should try to wean yourself from viewing secular television shows and movies. Set aside, perhaps, one night a month for a movie that is artistically beautiful and profound, or that in some way commemorates the sacred. Informative and edifying documentaries can make for excellent viewing. Always judge content with these questions: Does it promote the good? Is it truthful? Is it beautiful?

People waste much time on the Internet and electronic devices. If you can, restrict your access to the computer, email, and social media. View only the websites that you must as a student, or those that assist you in fulfilling your duties of state. Anything that takes up too much time or leaves you feeling anxious or agitated should be avoided. You have no need to be perusing celebrity gossip sites, online games, or political pundit blogs. If you have trouble restricting your social media use, then delete your accounts. If you spend too much time on the Internet then install a program that cuts off your access at certain times of the day or night.

Internal silence is more complicated and not so easily obtained. Internal silence means restraint in one's thought, imagination, and emotions so that one can be attuned to the movements of God in one's soul. It is necessary for holiness and cannot be obtained without mortification and prayer.

It is God Himself who teaches and brings interior silence to a soul, but the soul must be open to being taught. It must routinely sit with God in prayer (daily prayer, regular Eucharistic Adoration, etc.) and it must make sacrifices to predispose itself to this silence.

Examples of various sacrifices or mortifications include:

- the imposition of exterior silence as discussed above;
- keeping yourself busy and on schedule according to your plan of life so that your mind doesn't have the opportunity to indulge in self-absorbed pondering;
- restriction of speech: not speaking ill of others, not speaking of one's troubles, not speaking about this or that topic unless necessary.

If you are in doubt of what I write here, then consider the words of Saint Faustina:

God does not give Himself to a chattering soul, which, like a drone in a beehive, buzzes around but gathers no honey. A talkative soul is empty inside. It lacks both the essential virtues and intimacy with God. A deeper interior life, one of gentle peace and of that silence where the Lord dwells, is quite out of the question. A soul that has never tasted the sweetness of inner silence is a restless spirit, which disturbs the silence of others.[81]

Your confessor will guide you in this.

Mortification

Saint Paul introduces us to the idea of mortification:

If you live a life of nature, you are marked out for death; if you *mortify* the ways of nature through the power of the Spirit, you will have life. (Rom 8:13)[82]

Mortification is the voluntary "subjection and denial of bodily passions and appetites by abstinence or self-inflicted pain or discomfort"[83] so as to conform and subordinate them to "the rule of reason and faith, as discerned by the mind."[84]

Although mortification might appear to be something negative, its end is entirely positive. Denying oneself certain indulgences or enforcing certain restrictions is intended to strengthen the will. It will help you develop a habit of sacrifice

---

[81] *Diary*, no. 118.

[82] Emphasis added. The translation I use here is from the Knox Bible. The translation from the Navarre Bible, which I rely on elsewhere, is as follows: "for if you live according to the flesh you will die, but if by the Spirit you put to death the deeds of the body you will live." See also Colossians 3:5 and Galatians 5:24.

[83] *Merriam-Webster*, s.v. "mortification."

[84] *The Catholic Encyclopedia: An International Work of Reference on the Constitution, Doctrine, Discipline, and History of the Catholic Church* (New York: Appleton, 1911), s.v. "mortification."

and self-discipline so that you can grow in virtue. This will aid you in overcoming self-love and self-preference so that you can consistently love others through the free gift of yourself.

One way to think about mortification is to picture an athlete. An athlete trains regularly and imposes repetitious physical exercises over and over again to strengthen the body and will. All this is done to improve her performance at a meet or competition. In other words, you must train and strengthen your will so that when it really counts, you can be generous; you can exercise self-restraint; you can choose virtue over vice; you can serve rather than be served; you can be kind rather than unkind; you can forsake yourself for the good of others. Mortification "does not destroy but elevates nature."[85]

It is inadvisable to take on strenuous physical mortifications in the beginning stages of the spiritual life. Your day will provide you with many opportunities to mortify yourself: taking on small domestic chores we find distasteful, cheerfully bearing daily frustrations and disappointments, being kind and patient with a difficult colleague at school or work. The list is endless!

Additional mortifications you might consider when appropriate include:

+ Forgoing coffee, tea, or soft drinks except on Sundays
+ No meat on Fridays throughout the year (not just in Lent)
+ No meat on Wednesdays

---

[85] Ibid.

+ Fasting on Wednesdays and Fridays (and traditional Ember days)
+ No sweets or treats except Sunday
+ No seasoning on your food except on Sundays (a mortification practiced by Blessed Miriam Teresa Demjanovich)[86]
+ Be the first to jump up and do an unpleasant but necessary task
+ Turning the water cold at the end of every shower
+ Having only cold showers except on Sundays
+ Not using a snooze alarm. Get up and out of bed at the time you should
+ Going to bed on time
+ Not eating between meals
+ When saying the rosary, choosing a set of rosary beads that you don't find attractive (giving the beads you like best to someone else)
+ Opting to use the Missal or prayer book that is most worn or unattractive to you

Be judicious in which practices you adopt. If you find yourself feeling proud then choose something humble—opt for something that you won't want to boast about. If you have struggled with an eating disorder or disordered body image then don't do any of the mortifications related to food. It is important to practice temperance and prudence even in how you mortify yourself!

One way of ensuring temperance is to seek the guidance of your confessor as to the mortifications you take on. Try to

---

[86] Sister Mary Zita Geis, *Sister Miriam Teresa Demjanovich*, 87.

be obedient to his advice. If you are told not to undertake a strenuous mortification, then don't. You will please God more with your humility.

Annual Retreat

Make a point of going on retreat at least once a year. Spiritual retreats give us a beautiful opportunity to connect with Our Lord, to seek solace from the agitations of modern life, and to take stock of where we are and where we should be in our spiritual lives.[87] They are a very important part of the discernment process, and essential to eking out our sanctity in this busy world.

A led retreat is typically, although not necessarily, guided by a priest. The priest may give a series of lectures or conferences to guide you in your meditation and prayer. Ideally he will also hear your confession and provide you with spiritual direction. On an unled retreat, you are more or less on your own. A retreat like this will often involve staying in the guest house of a convent or monastery where you spend your time in silent prayer, joining the sisters or monks for their daily Mass and liturgies (the Divine Office).

Fulfillment of Duties of State

What are your "duties of state"? One's "duties of state" are the ordinary obligations and duties associated with one's primary state in life—as a parent, child, student, spouse, priest, religious, etc. Every Catholic must pray and attend Sunday Mass, for example, but we each have an additional set of obligations based on our current position and role. Our duties of state are

---

[87] Ibid.

both horizontal (owed to our fellow man) and vertical (owed to God). Fulfilling our duties of state with love and perseverance will help us become saints.

Your current duties of state are determined by your status as "student" and "daughter." Make sure that you attend your college classes on time. Pay attention to your professors. Be kind and polite, try to get your class reading done on time, and complete your assignments and exams to the best of your ability. Allocate an appropriate amount of time to study, and offer all of this work to God. Be kind and loving to your parents and siblings.

I strongly recommend that you read Jean-Charles Nault's book, *The Noonday Devil*, which will encourage and aid you in diligently fulfilling your duties of state.

Obedience

Saint Thomas Aquinas tells us that obedience is part of and necessary for the obtainment of religious perfection. He explains that "religious perfection consists chiefly in the imitation of Christ" and that "in Christ obedience is commended above all according to Philip. ii. 8. He became obedient unto death."[88]

Try to discipline your will and self-love by practicing cheerful obedience to your confessor. I do *not* mean by this that you should be blindly obedient, but that you should

---

[88] *ST* II-II, q. 186, a. 5. According to Saint Thomas Aquinas, "the vow of obedience is chief of the three religious vows" because "by the vow of obedience man offers God something greater, namely his own will; for this is of more account than his own body, which he offers God by continence, and then external things, which he offers God by poverty" (*ST* II-II, q. 186, a. 8).

approach your confessor with a thoughtful willingness to co-operate with and be guided by his advice. Ask questions but be open to what he has to say. This is important if you wish to make progress in the spiritual life and avoid common but devastating setbacks.

Study

Get to know God more deeply by reading His Word in the Sacred Scriptures. We cannot properly love Him if we do not know Him. God speaks to us through the Scriptures and tells us who He is.

Start with the Gospels. Allocate some time each day to reading a chapter. Within a year, you'll have read the entire New Testament.[89] Consider reading the Book of Psalms after that.

You should also know the teachings of our Faith. A good place to start is the Catechism. You might also study the writings of the early Church Fathers and Saint Thomas Aquinas. Saint Augustine is also important.

Those who are new converts to the Faith or who have had a reversion back to the Catholic faith of their childhood would benefit from reading *The Faith Explained* by Leo J. Trese.

You should also learn about the spiritual life. Draw up a reading list and work your way through this list. Read the works of Saint Teresa of Ávila, Saint John of the Cross, and Saint Thérèse of Lisieux. Read also the writings of Saint Francis de Sales and Saint Alphonus Liguori.

---

[89] Make sure the Bible you read is an approved translation. Have your confessor check that the version you select is unproblematic. It is also prudent to be reading an approved commentary at the same time.

In addition to being a college student, Blessed Pier Giorgio Frassati was a student of the Faith. While he worked towards a degree in engineering, he also studied Scripture, delved into Thomism, read the various encyclicals, and learned about the spiritual life. It was, as his sister later wrote, his "secret wisdom":

> He had got hold of the Epistles translated by Ramorino. . . . He read them on the tram or in the street, and, to anyone who wanted to know what was in the book, he said, "words of eternal life." The family knew almost nothing about his secret wisdom. He read St. Augustine, and some of the writings of St. Thomas Aquinas, whose *Summa Theologica* he was beginning to study. His favorite gospel was Matthew's because of the Sermon on the Mount. His favorite theme was that of the encyclical *Rerum Novarum*. He knew Pope Innocent III's *De Contemptu Mundi* and shared its contempt for riches and its love of the poor. He knew Veuillot's Testament by heart. He was enthusiastic about the Psalms. He also read Heine and Goethe to enrich his spiritual gifts.[90]

If you are interested in a particular order, then spend some time learning about that order. Read their rule. Read the writings or biography of their founder and those of other important saints within the order.

If Latin, Greek, or Hebrew are offered at your college,

---

[90] Luciana Frassati, *A Man of the Beatitudes: Pier Giorgio Frassati* (San Francisco: Ignatius Press, 1993), 139.

consider studying these as part of your undergraduate degree. If you think you might be called to a missionary order, then select a modern language or two as part of your course work.

In addition to all this, you may wish to receive some basic instruction in singing, especially in Gregorian chant.[91] The Second Vatican Council recognized the primacy of Gregorian chant in the Church's liturgical life: "The Church acknowledges Gregorian chant as characteristically belonging to the Roman liturgy, with the result that . . . all things being equal, Gregorian chant takes possession of the first place."[92] Sacred chant is not a mere aesthetic adornment to the liturgy and our prayer, but a way of placing the entire self—body, intellect, and soul—at the service of the liturgy. Chant is an integral part of our Catholic heritage, and religious orders have been pivotal in its development and preservation.

Today, there are many female religious communities utilizing chant in their daily liturgical life, including the Benedictine Sisters of Mary, Queen of Apostles near Gower, MO; the Benedictine Sisters of St. Scholastica Priory in Petersham, MA; the Carmels of Jesus, Mary and Joseph in Lincoln, NE and Elysburg, PA; and the Dominican Sisters of Mary, Mother of the Eucharist, in Ann Arbor, MI, to name but a few. Some of these communities have made recordings of their liturgical prayer. You can listen to them and, in this way, pray with the sisters as you discern.

---

[91] It is possible to chant the psalms, which make up the Divine Office, and to chant the Ordo of Holy Mass. Likewise, many beautiful hymns of the Church's sacred music tradition have been translated into the vernacular with their original melodies—Adoro Te Devote, Stabat Mater, O Salutaris Hostia, the Kyrie, Gloria, Credo, Sanctus, and Agnus Dei.

[92] *Sacrosanctum concilium*, §116.

Service

Our love for God must express itself in our love for others. We live out this love in a tangible way whenever we engage in spiritual or corporal works of mercy.

What are the spiritual and corporal works of mercy? "The *works of mercy* are charitable actions by which we come to the aid of our neighbor in his spiritual or bodily necessities" (CCC 2447). The spiritual works of mercy pertain to the spiritual needs of others while the corporal acts of mercy concern their physical or material needs. "Corporal," of course, comes from the Latin word "corpus," meaning body. The spiritual and corporal acts of mercy are listed in Table 1.[93]

One way to ensure that you regularly engage in spiritual and corporal works of mercy is by committing to a weekly or monthly form of service. Once a month, for example, you might assist at a soup kitchen run by the Missionaries of Charity. Alternatively, once a week you might teach English to immigrants or tutor children in a poor neighborhood. You could also volunteer at a crisis pregnancy center or homeless shelter for women and children.

For the spiritual works of mercy, consider teaching catechesis at your local parish or joining a pro-life group in which you commit to regular times of prayer in Eucharistic Adoration or outside an abortion clinic to obtain grace and conversion for women considering abortion and for the protection of their unborn children.

---

[93] The lists are based on that contained in the Catechism of the Catholic Church and the *Catholic Encyclopedia*. It is usual to phrase "ransom the captive" as "visit the imprisoned." I have chosen to include "ransom the captive" because modern slavery, human trafficking, and abortion are significant and widespread issues that should be of immense concern to us as Christians. We should work diligently to ransom these captives.

In choosing a form of service, consider the talents and gifts with which God has endowed you. Ask yourself: "How can I—with my particular talents, experience, and sensibilities—best be of service to others? What areas of Christian service am I naturally drawn to? What concerns me? What inspires me? What do I enjoy? What am I good at?" This exercise will also aid you in discerning which order you might be called to join.

Table 1: The Spiritual and Corporal Works of Mercy

Spiritual Works of Mercy	Corporal Works of Mercy
Instruct the ignorant	Feed the hungry
Counsel the doubtful	Give drink to the thirsty
Admonish sinners	Clothe the naked
Bear wrongs patiently	Shelter the homeless
Forgive offenses willingly	Visit the sick
Comfort the afflicted	Ransom the captive (or visit the imprisoned)
Pray for the living and the dead	Bury the dead

READING LIST

Study

+ Catechism of the Catholic Church
+ Leo J. Trese, *The Faith Explained*
+ A. G. Sertillanges, O.P., *The Intellectual Life: Its Spirit, Conditions, Methods*

Sacraments

- Leonard of Port Maurice, *The Hidden Treasure: Holy Mass*
- Reginald Garrigou-Lagrange, O.P., *The Three Ages of the Interior Life: Prelude of Eternal Life*:
  - Part 2, Chapter 30: "Sacramental Confession"
  - Part 2, Chapter 31: "Assistance at Mass, the Source of Sanctification"
  - Part 2, Chapter 32: "Holy Communion"
  - Part 3, Chapter 24: "The Sacrifice of the Mass and Proficients"
  - Part 3, Chapter 25: "The Communion of Proficients"
- Francis Randolph, *Know Him in the Breaking of the Bread: A Guide to the Mass*

Prayer

- *Handbook of Prayers*, Scepter Press/Midwest Theological Forum
- Brett A. Brannen, *To Save a Thousand Souls*
  - Chapter 6: "Developing a Spiritual Plan of Life"
  - Chapter 8: "Hearing the Voice of God"
- Jean-Baptiste Chautard, O.C.S.O, *The Soul of the Apostolate*
- Francis de Sales, *Introduction to the Devout Life*
- Aurora Griffin, *How I Stayed Catholic at Harvard* (for students)
- Alphonsus Liguori, *How to Converse With God*
- Jacques Philippe, *Time for God*
- Teresa of Ávila, *Life*

Divine Office

+ UK: *Morning and Evening Prayer: With Night Prayer from the Divine Office* (Collins, part of HarperCollins Publishers)
+ US: *Shorter Christian Prayer: The Four-Week Psalter of the Liturgy of the Hours Containing Morning Prayer and Evening Prayer with Selections for the Entire Year* (Catholic Book Publishing Co.)
+ Reginald Garrigou-Lagrange, O.P., *The Three Ages of the Interior Life: Prelude of Eternal Life*, Part 2, Chapter 34: "Liturgical Prayer"

Duties of State

+ Aurora Griffin, *How I Stayed Catholic at Harvard* (for students)
+ Jean-Charles Nault, *The Noonday Devil: Acedia, the Unnamed Evil of Our Times*

Mortification

+ Reginald Garrigou-Lagrange, O.P., *The Three Ages of the Interior Life: Prelude of Eternal Life*, Part 2, Chapter 20: "Mortification According to St. Paul and the Reasons for Its Necessity"

Chant: CDs

+ *Mater Eucharistiae*, Dominican Sisters of Mary, Mother of the Eucharist
+ *Voices: Chant from Avignon*, Benedictine Sisters of Le Barroux
+ *Advent at Ephesus*, Benedictine Sisters of Ephesus
+ *Lent at Ephesus*, Benedictine Sisters of Ephesus

+ *Easter at Ephesus,* Benedictine Sisters of Ephesus
+ *Viens en Paix Marie,* The Monastic Family of Bethlehem of the Assumption of the Virgin and of Saint Bruno

Chant: Resources

+ Church Music Association of America: http://musicasacra.com
+ *How to Read and Sing Gregorian Chant:* http://www.ccwatershed.org/Gregorian/

Ascending the Mountain

Dear Marie Therese,

We spoke tonight of how the spiritual life is like a mountain that one must climb. There is a gradation to the spiritual life—it is not flat terrain.

We are called always to be growing in holiness—to climb ever higher on the path of perfection. It is not simply a matter of black and white, sin or no sin, holy or unholy.

Yes, of course, someone is either in a state of grace or they are not. Here we do have a sharp dichotomy. But this—so to speak—is the base camp of the spiritual life. It is the beginning. The very start is to be free of mortal sin. There is then a steep, long, and arduous road to be climbed. See Illustration 1.

If holiness were simply a matter of respecting the Commandments, Our Lord would not have given us the Beatitudes (Matthew 5:1–12). While the Ten Commandments impose negative restraints on our behavior, the Beatitudes are positive commands, which can never be perfectly or completely fulfilled while we are here on earth.[94] We can almost always practice them more perfectly, more consistently, and more lovingly.

Another way to think about this is to imagine a potted plant. The container holds and protects the plant—it allows the plant to receive the water and fertilizer it needs to live and grow. When the container is broken or shattered, the plant

---

[94] With the exception, of course, of Our Lord, Our Lady, and likely Saint Joseph.

can't take in or retain the water or nutrients it needs, and the plant dies or is stunted.

In the spiritual life, God also gives us a "container" to protect our souls. This container is the Decalogue and the Precepts of the Church. They provide a moral and spiritual framework or structure within which we can grow in holiness.

Respecting the Ten Commandments and the law of the Church allows our souls to remain free from mortal sin. If the integrity of this framework is compromised—that is, if, like a container, it is cracked (venial sin) or shattered (mortal sin), the soul cannot take in the water and nutrients (grace from the sacraments) it needs to survive and flourish.

Having an intact container is, however, just the beginning. The intact container means that the plant can receive the water and nutrients it needs to grow—it has more work and growth to do to become the plant God created it to be. In a similar way, our souls have much work to do to grow in holiness. When the spiritual framework of our soul is intact, the soul can grow and cooperate with the graces it receives by spending time in prayer, living the Beatitudes, and practicing charity.

The growth in virtue can be great or small depending on the graces that the soul receives and how receptive she is to those graces. In time, the soul might grow to be a precious, spiritual violet like Saint Thérèse or a large, strong tree like Saint Paul.

Are you ready and willing to ascend the Mountain of Perfection?

Illustration 1: Climbing the Mountain of God

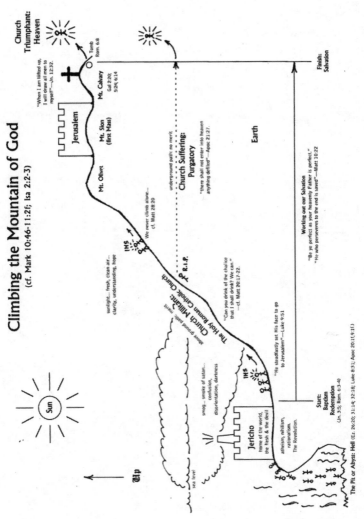

Illustration by Fr. Joannes Petrus

❧

Evil

Dear Marie Therese,

The devil achieves many victories by concealing himself. Skeptics do not believe that he exists. Their spiritual blindness gives him great influence over them.

As you advance in the spiritual life and begin to do battle against your more hidden faults (self-love, lack of detachment, pride, etc.), Satan will attack you in more obvious ways.

In periods of aridity, he may subtly suggest to you that you are right to doubt: that it is ridiculous to believe such and such dogma or teaching of the Church, that you should not bother doing all these prayers, and so on.

During periods of darkness, he may whisper to you that God does not love you, that God has abandoned you, or worse.

Sometimes he may bring up impure memories, thoughts, or temptations. When such images or thoughts seem to rise up out of nowhere, they might be of demonic origin.

One way to remedy this is to immediately call out to Jesus: *"Jesus, please, by your Holy name, bind these spirits at the foot of your cross"* or, simply, *"Help me dear Jesus!"* If it is a diabolical attack, you should have immediate relief.

Sometimes Satan's attacks will not be subtle and are designed to frighten and cow you, to undermine your faith in God's love, protection, and mercy. Padre Pio was physically attacked by demons in his cell at night. Saint Gemma and Saint John Vianney were similarly tormented.

One day, after adoring Our Lord in the Blessed Sacrament, Saint Faustina was surrounded by a huge pack of dogs who were jumping and howling, and trying to tear her apart:

> I realized that they were not dogs but demons. One of them spoke up in a rage, "Because you have snatched so many souls away from us this night, we will tear you to pieces." I answered, "If that is the will of the most merciful God, tear me to pieces, for I have justly deserved it, because I am the most miserable of all sinners, and God is ever holy, just, and infinitely merciful." To these words all the demons answered as one, "Let us flee, for she is not alone; the Almighty is with her!" And they vanished like dust, like the noise of the road, while I continued on my way to my cell undisturbed, finishing my *Te Deum* and pondering the infinite and unfathomable mercy of God.[95]

The main thing to remember is that this battle is not won in the usual way that battles are won. That is, it is not won by direct confrontation.

We are very little compared to angelic creatures—little in intelligence, resolve, and will. As your father wisely tells you, "Don't match wits with the devil." You will lose.

Rather, this battle is won by letting Christ and His mother fight and win it for you. God will always prevail. You do your part by simply recognizing and accepting your littleness and your ability to do almost nothing in the face of evil but cling—like a child—to Jesus.

Satan and the demons do not understand humility and

---

[95] *Diary*, no. 320

cannot comprehend how suffering can be joyfully accepted and turned into something beautiful for God. This is how you defeat them: humility and acceptance. Accepting this cross from God and humbly relying on God rather than your own efforts to conquer this very scary and formidable foe.

Protect yourself with the Brown Scapular (the Scapular of Our Lady of Mount Carmel) and Saint Benedict's medal, say the Saint Michael prayer daily, and stick to your regular routine of prayer, Confession, and Holy Mass.

Reading List

+ Gabriele Amorth, *An Exorcist Tells His Story*
+ Timothy Gallagher, O.M.V., *The Discernment of Spirits*

THE TABERNACLE OF YOUR HEART
AND HOME

Dear Marie Therese,

You have had the great fortune of living at home with your parents during your college years.

It is an unusual choice to make in this part of the world (although not elsewhere), and I know that it was a sacrifice for you. Try to think of it, however, as a gift from Our Lord.

First, Jesus is asking you to be home—just as He was with Mary and Joseph for the duration of His hidden life. Jesus did not go away for college. He lived out His rabbinic knowledge and practiced His carpentry trade at home. He is asking you to be like Him. He wants this part of your life to mimic the corresponding part of His life. He is asking you—His beloved—to share in His hidden life. What a beautiful gift! What a beautiful opportunity to know Him more fully and follow Him in this way. Thank God for this. It is an unusual and seldom appreciated gift.

Second, Our Lord is using these circumstances to protect and nurture you. Your parents love and support you in your discernment. They have a solid Christian marriage and are able to provide you with a safe, stable, supportive, and nurturing home within which you can undertake the work of discernment and preparation.

You will be protected from all sorts of threats and harms to your virtue, physical safety, intellectual integrity, and spiritual development simply by living at home with loving and sensible parents.

A certain amount of stability is beneficial at this point in your spiritual life. You need a somewhat dependable routine as well as time and space to pray and the ability to attend Mass and Confession. Your parents will assist you in this.

Think of your parents' home as a nest. Return to it each day and take shelter. Rest in it and garner the strength you need to venture forth into the world to do your work as a student and undertake the spiritual preparation of a pre-vocation religious soul.

Another way of thinking about your parents' home and marriage is to imagine it as a tabernacle.

Our Lord allows Himself to be locked up in the tabernacle. There He is safe from vandals while in such a vulnerable state. There He is available to us at all hours. He is free to receive us despite His containment.

Likewise, Christ is offering you protection in the tabernacle of your parents' home. Here you are removed and hidden from the world. He is there with you. Draw close to Him in your family life.

Family life gives us so many opportunities to serve. If you are called to religious life, your family life will be a precursor to the type of communal life you'll experience in the convent.

By entering a convent you will imitate Our Lord in the Blessed Sacrament in three ways. First, physically: you allow yourself to be contained within the physical confines of the convent building similar to the way in which Our Lord allows Himself to be locked within the physical structure of the tabernacle. This will be most obvious if you join an enclosed, contemplative order. Second, relationally: your vows lock you into a community or religious family with whom you serve God and grow in holiness. This is a relational confinement that mimics not only His confinement in the physical tabernacle but also the way in which Our Lord makes Himself available through the Blessed Sacrament to those belonging to His Mystical Body in a gift of supreme, parental, loving exclusivity. Third, spiritually: a religious vocation binds your soul to Him and to no other. Your path to Him is contained within your vocation, and you dwell with Him by living out your vocation. The confinement of your vocation frees you to be with Him more perfectly.

By emulating Christ in the tabernacle, religious open themselves to a river of grace. Christ is eager to love and bless those who emulate Him in the Blessed Sacrament in this way.

A woman and man "wed-lock" themselves into their sacramental marriage in a similar though less obvious way. Through the Sacrament of Marriage, the man and woman come to mimic the Blessed Sacrament. First, together, as a unity, they embody their sacrament. Second, as a couple they live their sacramental calling and it (their marriage) becomes nourishment (like the Blessed Sacrament) for the children given to the union. Third, the physical home they provide for one another and their children acts like a physical tabernacle within which hearts and souls can be nurtured for Christ. Such sacramental "locking" frees and nourishes the soul. We are contained, protected, and nourished within the sacrament.

Enclosing yourself within the protective tabernacle of your parents' home and the graces of their sacramental marriage (and then again in the convent) will help you prepare your heart as a ciborium.

Within the protective tabernacles of our families (religious or natural) we are called to fashion our souls into living ciboria. The prior steps and enclosures (physical, relational, and vocational or sacramental tabernacles) are preparation for this. In other words, the relational, physical, and spiritual enclosures in which we hide ourselves allow God to enter and—in a hidden way—transform our souls into hidden ciboria. Because marriage and the religious life involve every aspect of our being—our bodies, souls, intellect, will, imagination, *and* emotions—He is able to transform the entirety of our being when we enter—fully and faithfully—into our vocational (religious life) or sacramental (marriage) tabernacles.

God chooses to take some souls a little further and, with their cooperation and consent, He fashions the soul into a monstrance, which He then holds up so that the entire world can see Him glorified in and adored by that soul (Padre Pio and Mother Teresa are examples).

None of this is possible, however, unless we first enter into the hidden life with Our Lord.

Ask Jesus to make your heart into a living ciborium in which He can dwell.

Ask God to give you the grace to love and desire the hidden life.

Keep Good Company

Dear Marie Therese,

I cannot stress enough the importance of choosing virtuous friends.

Mother Teresa of Calcutta was only a young girl when she learned the importance of having good companions. Her mother placed a rotten apple in a bowl of fresh, ripe apples and had the young saint observe how, over time, the rot of the bad apple eventually spread and destroyed the good apples.[96]

Bad friendships are very much like this. Instead, we need to surround ourselves with women who love God and who are trying to be holy if we want to be good and holy ourselves.

Most friendships are what can be termed *natural*. They are based on worldly or external considerations—you might be friends because you happen to be the same age, happen to live in the same neighborhood, happen to like the same music, or happen to know the same people. These are friendships rooted in accidentals. Many will pass, others will mature but will be limited to common interests.

The superior friendship is *supernatural*. These friendships are based on and rooted in Christ. Such friends are companion souls with whom you journey up the mountain of sanctity. Supernatural friendships are gifts from God. They are not all that common but they are invaluable and beautiful.

Supernatural friendships are a must—especially at the

---

[96] Kathryn Spink, *Mother Teresa: A Complete Authorized Biography* (New York: HarperCollins, 1997), 7.

beginning of the spiritual life. Later on God might ask you to detach yourself even from these friendships, but at the beginning they are necessary to sustain you and keep you on the right track.

Do not mistake the benefits that a supernatural friendship will provide with the joys of your less fertile, natural friendships. Surround yourself with women who are trying to love God and grow in holiness; women who aspire to virtue will help you grow in virtue. Choose friends with good habits whose speech and conduct reflect pure hearts and minds.

Yes, evangelization is important but you must not do it at the risk of being co-opted by friends who take you away from God. Treat everyone with love and respect but be wary of emotional intimacy and dependency on worldly women.

The point to remember here is that you are trying to discern and prepare for religious life. Unless you are like Saint Teresa of the Andes (and most likely you are not), this is just the beginning of a long, beautiful but arduous journey in which you will need prayers and friends who sustain and encourage you in your ascent up the spiritual mountain. Be wary of friends who are a bad influence!

Ask Saint Teresa of the Andes to intercede for you in this matter. Saint Teresa had a gift for holy friendship and was able to bring many of those she loved (including the lukewarm or lapsed) closer to Jesus. She is a superb role model for you. Emulate her and ask her for help!

READING LIST

+ Hugh Black, *The Art of Being a Good Friend*
+ Michael Griffin, *God, the Joy of My Life: A Biography of Saint Teresa of Jesus of the Andes*
+ Jennifer Moorcroft, *God is All Joy: The Life of St. Teresa of the Andes*
+ Saint Teresa of the Andes, *Letters of Saint Teresa of Jesus of the Andes*

Dating

Dear Marie Therese,

Under no circumstances should you be dating.

Your discernment is a form of courtship and during this period you should focus on Jesus. You might find it helpful to give yourself a time frame within which you will "date" Jesus. Say to yourself: "For the next six (or 12 or 18) months I'm going to give my time and emotions to Jesus and I'll see where He takes me. And I'm not going to date anyone else!"

Dating during discernment is a common mistake, and it was one that even Saint Teresa of the Andes made. Her biographer tells us that:

> When Saint Teresa of the Andes was still a schoolgirl, she told a Sacred Heart sister at her school about a *pololeo*, or flirtation, she'd developed with a boy. When the sister pointed out that having a boyfriend was incompatible with a vocation to religious life, Saint Teresa quickly and courageously chose to prioritize her discernment and vocation.[97]

Also, know that dating can induce an emotional attachment to a person (even if the courtship is chaste), which will cloud your ability to freely discern what God is asking of you. A large part of the discernment and preparation process is gradual detachment—from worldly things, from others, from

---

[97] Moorcroft, *God is All Joy*, 28.

vice and sin, from one's preferences, and so on—so that you can respond promptly and immediately to God's call.

Dating will make this very difficult. Sometimes you will hear of people who break off an engagement to enter into the priesthood or religious life. This is different. In these cases, the person thinks (in good faith despite, perhaps, occasional feelings of unease) that they should enter into marriage. God intervenes in a dramatic fashion to claim the soul as His own. This is not your situation.

Dating can also give rise to occasions of sin or worse. You cannot do the job of discerning and preparing for religious life if you have to do constant battle trying to preserve your purity. Modern "dating" often introduces occasions of sin, which make it difficult to preserve one's purity. Falling into sins of impurity can lead not only to the loss of grace (in the case of mortal sin) but also the loss of a vocation.

If you do enter religious life after dating, any imprudent or unchaste actions, discussions, or choices you made while dating will remain in your memory and can taint your imagination. Try to give your religious life the best possible foundation by avoiding all dating while in the preparation and discernment period.

Dating during discernment is also selfish and shows a lack of charity for others. When I was a young, single woman, it was not unheard of for men in the "Catholic singles" community to date women while concurrently discerning a vocation to the priesthood.

What a poor way to treat Jesus! What a poor way to treat the women they took out on dates! A person who dates while discerning shows a lack of prudence and charity towards others, obliviousness to scandal, and a dearth of resilience. Let this not be you!

This is another issue that Saint Teresa of the Andes can assist you with. Do not hesitate to entrust this part of your discernment and preparation to her.

DISCRETION

Dear Marie Therese,

You asked me the other day why Father W. recommends that those in discernment not tell others that they think they might have a calling to the priesthood or religious life. He does so because there is a danger that people will try to sway you one way or the other.

There are other reasons for this wise advice.

First, here are three pitfalls you can avoid by maintaining silence about your discernment and preparation:

i. *Pride*: when you speak of discernment and a desire for religious life, others will become excited for you and many will start to look up to you. They will esteem you. Their words of praise may undermine—without grace from God—your humility. You may come to enjoy the attention, and this will distract you from honest discernment.

ii. *Discouragement*: others will think poorly either of you or the religious life, and will try to dissuade you from preparing for it. They will tell you that you will be wasting your life. Or they will undermine your trust in Jesus by criticizing you: by pointing out all your flaws, and questioning why Jesus would call you for this. It is not for them to judge. Jesus will call whomever He chooses. Think of Saint Mary Magdalene and Saint Margaret of Cortona in these moments, and ask for their intercession. Do not allow yourself to be discouraged. Ignore uninformed commentary on religious life, and try not to open yourself to such conversations in the first place.

iii. *Scandal*: the faithful who know and support you will be filled with much hope and gratitude to God at the news of your entry into religious life. Conversely, if they find out about your discernment too soon, some will be disappointed and discouraged if you do not enter. It is an act of charity to protect them somewhat from this.

Second, by wrapping your discernment in a protective blanket of silence, you imitate Our Lady in her perfection.

Think of the example given by Our Lady following the Annunciation and birth of Our Lord: "*But Mary kept all these things, pondering them in her heart*" (Luke 2:19).[98] She receives the amazing events of the Incarnation and birth of Our Lord with restraint (visits by foreign kings and angelically instructed shepherds!) and responds with even more restraint and prayer.

After the Annunciation, Our Lady did not tell people about her "calling" or discuss what passed between her and the angel. She did not announce her pregnancy or the manner in which it occurred. She was not self-involved, proud, or chatty.

---

[98] I have used the Navarre Bible for most scriptural quotes in this book. Other translations express Luke 2:19 as follows: "*But Mary treasured up all these things and pondered them in her heart.*" This second translation is in some ways more instructive: like Mary we should *treasure* in our hearts the supernatural gifts and graces we receive from God. Treasure is something we should be careful with—it is not something to be squandered.

Saint Elizabeth was not told about it by Mary but received an interior light and understanding:

> In those days Mary arose and went with haste into the hill country, to a city of Judah and she entered the house of Zechariah and greeted Elizabeth, And when Elizabeth heard the greeting of Mary, the babe leaped in her womb; and Elizabeth was filled with the Holy Spirit and she exclaimed with a loud cry, "Blessed are you among women, and blessed is the fruit of your womb! And why is this granted me, that the mother of my Lord should come to me?" (Luke 1:39–43)

It is not wrong to talk with others about your discernment, but the way of perfection is the way of Mary. Follow her in her silence.

Saint Teresa of the Andes exercised superb discretion during her discernment. She went to great lengths to keep her discernment secret. Her efforts were, at times, sweet and endearingly comical. Here is an excerpt of a letter she wrote to her future mother superior at Carmel, instructing Mother on how to address the letters she sent to Teresa (then known as Juanita) so that they did not attract attention:

> Don't be surprised that I wasn't able to answer your letter immediately, because it's very difficult to write here because my father's in charge of dropping off letters in the mailbox. And I also beg that, when you write, please don't put Del Solar on the envelope, because "Del" will draw attention and then they'll start

asking me who's addressing me that way. And I'll go through a real mess trying to evade their questions, without lying. It's true, that we do have that last name, but we never use it in that way.[99]

I encourage you to learn about this sweet and joyful saint: read her letters and befriend her.

Ask Our Lady to intercede for you that you are given the great gift of silence.

READING LIST

+ Saint Teresa of the Andes, *Letters of Saint Teresa of Jesus of the Andes*
+ Jennifer Moorcroft, *God is All Joy: The Life of St. Teresa of the Andes*
+ Michael Griffin, *God, the Joy of My Life: A Biography of Saint Teresa of Jesus of the Andes*

---

[99] Teresa of the Andes to Mother Angelica Teresa, 22 January 1919, in *Letters*, 106–107. See also letter no. 62 for Teresa's delightful account of how she concealed the postulant's clothing Mother Angelica had sent for her to try on by hiding it under her jacket.

MODESTY

Dear Marie Therese,

As you enter into serious discernment and preparation for religious life, you should develop some healthy detachment about your dress and appearance. You already dress quite modestly. Continue to do so. Ask God to help you grow in this area—not just in dress but in speech and attitude too.[100]

Do not place undue importance on your appearance. Develop a love for the simple. Try to be frugal. Make do with what you have, and when you do need to acquire new clothes or shoes, favor quality and practicality over style. Avoid the ostentatious, and restrict yourself in terms of spending.

Take care to dress well for Jesus when you attend Mass. As a rule, tight or revealing clothing is a bad idea. Just as it is an act of charity to others to dress neatly, it is also an act of charity to dress in a way that doesn't attract too much or the wrong kind of attention to yourself while in discernment.[101] To be clear: I am not advocating dowdiness, frumpiness, or neglect of yourself or your appearance. On the contrary, the virtue of modesty is the knowledge and practice of what is "in measure" according to time, place, and person.[102]

One day Saint Francis de Sales saw Saint Jane Francis de Chantal better dressed than usual. She was then a young

---

[100] Modesty starts with our dress but we should also strive to be modest in our words, postures, actions, and thoughts.

[101] You might choose, for example, not to wear makeup, color your hair, or paint your nails as you prepare to enter religious life.

[102] *ST* II-II, q. 169.

widow and had not yet entered religious life. Saint Francis de Sales asked her, "Madam, do you wish to marry again?" When she replied, "No," he said, "Very well, but then you should pull down your flag."[103]

You'll find all this easier to do if you have a healthy understanding of your beauty and worth. Consider what it is that makes you beautiful to God. Many women, even faithful Catholic women, fall victim to the message that a woman's worth lies in her appearance.

Remember always that God loves you! He died on the Cross for you. You are a precious daughter of Christ and it is in this that you are most beautiful:

> Down deep we all know that clothing and jewelry are not the person. The individual in elegant evening dress is not one atom different from the same person in paint-smeared work clothes. The Christian is immeasurably more interested in the splendor of truth, the symphony of music, the beauty of nature and art, the glory of prayer and selfless human love. These are values no thief can reach, no moth destroy (Luke 12:33).[104]

Kitty, the central character in W. Somerset Maugham's novel *A Painted Veil*, sees but fails to understand the peace and hope she finds in the Catholic nuns she meets. Nevertheless, she recognizes that the nuns are beautiful and that this

---

[103] "St. Jane Frances de Chantal," in *Butler's Lives of the Saints*, 3:370.

[104] Thomas Dubay, *Happy Are You Poor: The Simple Life and Spiritual Freedom* (San Francisco: Ignatius Press, 1981), 121–122.

beauty is grounded in virtue and prayer:

> Your first thought when you looked at the Mother
> Superior was that as a girl she must have been beau-
> tiful, but in a moment you realized that this was a
> woman whose beauty, depending on character, had
> grown with advancing years.[105]

Some may not understand why you aim for detachment in
dress. They might feel uncomfortable and express their discomfort with criticism. When this occurs, consider the
example of Saint Gemma Galgani who consistently wore a
"uniform" of a black dress, black cape, and a large black hat.
She was always dressed neatly but was exceedingly modest,
and allowed little variety to her dress. When she received
the stigmata she also started to wear gloves. She was mocked
for this but remained unperturbed. There is a story that her
sister-in-law, offended that Saint Gemma wore gloves at the
dinner table while eating, tore them off Saint Gemma's hands
only to be shocked and contrite when she saw Saint Gemma's
stigmata.

Of course, if it becomes clear that God wishes for you to
enter the married state, you can put more effort into dressing
in a way that is both fashionable and modest. The following
quote has been attributed to Pope Pius XII:

> God does not ask us to live outside our times, to ig-
> nore the dictates of fashion to the point of becoming

---

[105] W. Somerset Maugham, *The Painted Veil* (New York: Vintage, 2006),
117.

ridiculous, dressing contrary to the tastes and habits common to our contemporaries, without ever worrying about their likes and dislikes. . . . What God asks is always to bear in mind that fashion is not, and cannot be, the supreme rule of conduct; that above fashion and its dictates there are higher and more imperious laws, superior and immutable principles, that can in no case be sacrificed to the whim of pleasure or caprice, and before which the idol of fashion must be ready to abdicate its fleeting omnipotence.[106]

Ask Our Lady to tutor you in modesty. Ask Saint Gemma to help you. Dress for God and for God alone.

Reading List
+ Thomas Dubay, *Happy Are You Poor: The Simple Life and Spiritual Freedom*
+ Saint Gemma Galgani, *Autobiography*
+ Fr. Germanus, *The Life of St. Gemma Galgani*
+ Pope Pius XII, *Sacra virginitas*
+ Thomas Aquinas, *Summa Theologica*, Part II-II, Question 169

---

[106] Pius XII, Address to the Delegation of Young Women of Catholic Action, May 22, 1941.

Hostile Environments

Dear Marie Therese,

You are very blessed to have the encouragement and support of your parents. Not everyone does. Many young women endure varying degrees of persecution on account of their Faith and desire to enter religious life.

Blessed Pier Giorgio Frassati was unappreciated and unloved by his family: "everyone at home wished he were different" and he was considered the "least important."[107] Family life was tense and miserable; his parents did not get along, his father was domineering and his mother harsh.[108] They ascribed his piety to "his low intelligence," and when he was dying, they didn't notice.[109] Days before his death, his mother complained, "Pier Giorgio could choose a better moment to be ill."[110] According to his sister, Luciana, "he died, misunderstood to the very end."[111]

If the persecution is mild, one should consider the example of Saint Catherine of Siena, who was greatly put upon by her family. When they tried to force her into marriage, she cut off her hair.[112] Failing to marry her off, they then forced her to serve the family as a menial laborer and sought to deprive her

---

[107] Luciana Frassati, *A Man of the Beatitudes*, 45, 63. See also p. 160.
[108] Ibid., 58–69.
[109] Ibid., 151.
[110] Ibid., 157.
[111] Ibid., 154.
[112] Sigrid Undset, *Catherine of Siena* (London: Sheed and Ward, 1954), 28.

of the silence and solitude she craved.[113] Saint Catherine's response and advice was to "build a cell inside your mind, from which you can never flee."[114]

How did she do this? Saint Elizabeth of the Trinity imitated Saint Catherine of Siena by praying to God, asking Him "to watch over her and keep her inwardly united with him" so that "she could keep her Lord company and, even in the midst of her daily life, keep her heart and her thoughts fixed on him."[115] You can do the same.

If the persecution turns into abuse (physical, verbal, or emotional), one should leave home.[116] In these cases, one ought to model Saint Faustina and her life in the year prior to her entry into the Sisters of Our Lady of Mercy. She fled her home and resided with a pious woman in Warsaw. For twelve months she lived a quiet, contemplative life, and labored as a domestic servant to earn the money she needed for her habit—all the while spiritually preparing for entry into religious life. She describes this period of her life as follows:

> At that time I had to struggle with many difficulties, but God was lavish with His graces. An ever-greater longing for God began to take hold of me. The lady, pious as she was, did not understand the happiness

---

[113] Ibid., 29.

[114] Ibid., 30.

[115] Jennifer Moorcroft, *He Is My Heaven: The Life of Elizabeth of the Trinity* (Washington, DC: ICS Publications, 2001), 16.

[116] I give this advice on the basis that you are no longer a minor. Consider living with an aunt or grandparent, if possible. Souls in the initial stages of the spiritual life usually aren't able to withstand the degree of persecution and abuse that more advanced souls, like Saint Catherine of Siena, can endure.

of religious life, and in her kindness began to make other plans for my future life. And yet, I sensed that I had a heart so big that nothing would be capable of filling it. And so I turned with all the longing of my soul to God.[117]

Thankfully, you are not experiencing rejection in your home or by your family. However, as you have already found, your desire for Christ will mean you are rejected elsewhere. I know that the rejection you are experiencing with your peers at college is painful.

Jesus is asking you to share in this part of His Passion. You spoke out in defense of life and Christian marriage, and your peers and professors now punish you for this. It is not a coincidence that you underwent this trial during Holy Week.

I know it is hard. Ask God for the grace to embrace this cross and trial. Ask God for the light to see what He is doing to your soul by these means, and how He is using this cross to strengthen you in detachment and virtue. In doing this you will find it easier to appreciate and even rejoice in your social rejection and isolation. You will begin to feel gratitude for this, both to God and to those who have rejected you.

Reading List

+ Walter Joseph Ciszek, S.J., *He Leadeth Me*
+ Walter Joseph Ciszek, S.J., *With God in Russia*

---

[117] *Diary*, no. 15.

HUMILIATIONS

Dear Marie Therese,

At the beginning of the spiritual life, it is easy for a person to feel that she has it all worked out. The soul, tickled by its growth and the emotional consolations it receives from God, delights in its progress and is susceptible to thinking it has achieved greater sanctity than it has.

If the soul is earnest in wanting to love God and grow in humility, God will slowly help it see its littleness and wretchedness—its complete dependency on God for any and all good that it does.

God does this by humbling the soul. He reveals to it its poverty and wretchedness.

He can do this through any number of means. Sometimes, though rarely, He gives it a great light so the soul sees instantly and very clearly its deficiency (either in its entirety or in relation to a particular area), and—being humbled so dramatically—she receives the grace to overcome this deficiency. This is what happened to Saint Paul.

God allows other souls to falter in their efforts to grow, and to be subject to humiliation. In doing so, He is then able to coax greater growth out of them.

Let me explain: the soul will often see a fault (let's say anger or impatience) and it will labor away, thinking that it is making great progress only to lose its temper or become impatient at a mere trifle. God repeatedly allows the soul to falter and stumble like this in order to humble it—so that it sees that it must become like a meek, helpless child who is strengthened only by God and who credits only God for this strengthening and subsequent increase in virtue.

Do not be surprised if—as you make strides in the spiritual life—your faults become apparent or more visible to others. Others will see your wretchedness and remind you of it. They will see you stumble and think poorly of you.

They act as a mirror that God puts before you to remind you of your faults and nothingness.

The soul sees itself reflected in the eyes, opinions, and judgments of others, and is frequently reminded this way of its weakness and general inability to do or achieve anything without God. The soul becomes aware of what a terrible ambassador it is for God and the Catholic faith—what a terrible witness it is for Christ.

In this way God consistently humbles the soul, teaching it slowly to see itself for what and how it truly is (poor, weak, and usually full of self-love and delusional pride). He pushes the soul away from self-reliance to reliance on Him. The soul learns to beg God for the graces it needs to overcome certain faults and begins to lessen in self-love (and grow in love for God and neighbor) because it sees itself more accurately.

Consider Saint Faustina, who despite receiving extraordinary graces from God, was often avoided and thought of poorly by her fellow sisters. When told by another sister to "get it out of your head . . . that the Lord Jesus might be communing in such an intimate way with such a miserable bundle of imperfections as you," she asked Jesus why He associated "with such wretched people as I." Our Lord responded, "Be at peace, My daughter, it is precisely through such misery that I want to show the power of My mercy."[118]

Saint Bernadette similarly suffered after entering religious life. The superiors were especially severe on Saint Bernadette and humiliated her often. While very ill, one superior abused Bernadette for failing to die, saying "you're nothing but a little fool."[119] Her Novice Mistress also complained, "I don't understand why the Blessed Virgin appeared to Bernadette. There are so many others so refined, so well bred . . . !"[120] The other novices, noting how sharp and severe their Novice Mistress was with Bernadette, used to say to themselves, "How lucky I am not to be Bernadette!"[121]

Unfortunately for Bernadette, the Superior General could also be very harsh. On the day of her profession—a day that should have been joyful and serene—the Superior General publicly humiliated Bernadette by telling the Bishop and an audience, which included Bernadette, that "This child is good for nothing. She would be a burden to any house we sent her to."[122]

When lesser humiliations occur to you, give great thanks to God. He is showing you much mercy. Ask Saint Bernadette and Our Lady of Lourdes to help you persevere.

---

[118] *Diary*, no. 133.

[119] Abbé François Trochu, *Saint Bernadette Soubirous 1844–1879* (Charlotte, NC: TAN Books, 1957), 266.

[120] Ibid., 277.

[121] Ibid., 279–280.

[122] Ibid., 291.

Dominant Defect

Dear Marie Therese,

Nothing in life will humble you more consistently than your dominant defect.

Your dominant defect is the fault or tendency that will keep you from God more than any other fault. For some it might be a tendency to anger; for others it might be sloth or selfishness:

> There are temperaments inclined to effeminacy, indolence, sloth, gluttony, and sensuality. Others are inclined especially to anger and pride. We do not all climb the same slope toward the summit of perfection: those who are effeminate by temperament must by prayer, grace, and virtue become strong; and those who are naturally strong, to the point of easily becoming severe, must, by working at themselves and by grace, become gentle.[123]

You need to know what your dominant defect is so that you can work against it. Without this self-knowledge you won't know what graces to ask for to overcome it, and you won't know which virtues you need to practice to counteract this tendency. In fact, Father Reginald Garrigou-Lagrange, O.P., goes so far as to say that without this knowledge, we can have

---

[123] Reginald Garrigou-Lagrange, O.P., *The Three Ages of the Interior Life: Prelude of Eternal Life*, 398–399.

no true interior life, likening it to a "devouring worm in a beautiful fruit."[124]

How can you discover what this fault is?

First, ask Jesus to help you see what your weaknesses are—most especially the predominant fault—and then ask Him for the grace to overcome it.

Second, consider what things you are naturally preoccupied with: "Toward what do my most ordinary preoccupations tend, in the morning when I awake, or when I am alone? Where do my thoughts and desires go spontaneously?"[125] What do your thoughts tend to dwell on? Are you overly concerned with injustices committed against you? Do you fixate on obtaining and experiencing certain comforts? If so, which comforts? Or do you find yourself strategizing to further your ambitions?

Third, consider what it is that most often leads you to sin: "What is generally the cause or source of my sadness and joy? What is the general motive of my actions, the ordinary origin of my sins, especially when it is not a question of an accidental sin, but rather a succession of sins or a state of resistance to grace, notably when this resistance persists for several days and leads me to omit my exercises of piety?"[126]

Finally, seek out the guidance and advice of your confessor and spiritual director. A confessor will often recognize the dominant defect before the penitent does and can help you devise a plan to overcome it.

Do not lose heart! We must be detached even from our

---

[124] Ibid., 400.
[125] Ibid., 401.
[126] Ibid.

own faults and, while sorrowing in them, rejoice that Christ's sacrifice has given us a way of overcoming them. He has set us free!

Reading List

+ Reginald Garrigou-Lagrange, O.P., *The Three Ages of the Interior Life: Prelude of Eternal Life*, Part 2, Chapter 22: "The Predominant Fault"

The Little Way of the Sinner: Offering God Our Failures

Dear Marie Therese,

God loves all of you and He wants all of you. This means that—whether you are called to religious life or not—He desires that you offer Him both your best and your worst. He cannot transform you in love until you give *everything* to Him.

We tend to want to offer God only what is good. But we must realize that we should give Him our faults and failures too. We can make offerings even of these!

If you feel discouraged by the fact you were distracted during Mass, then offer up both the distraction and your discouragement to Him. If you spoke poorly of another, offer the detraction as well as the disappointment you feel in yourself to Him. If you tripped up by complaining to someone about your problems or giving unsolicited advice, give these "falls" to Him. If you wasted time on the internet, offer this too.

Saint Maximilian Kolbe advises that we offer even our guilt to Mary:

> Whenever you feel guilty, even if it is because you have consciously committed a sin, a serious sin, something you have kept doing many, many times, never let the devil deceive you by allowing him to discourage you. Whenever you feel guilty, offer all your guilt to the Immaculate, without analyzing it or examining it, as something that belongs to her. . . .

My beloved, may every fall, even if it is serious and habitual sin, always become for us a small step toward a higher degree of perfection.[127]

If Saint Thérèse's spirituality was "the little way" then this can be thought of as the *little way of the sinner*. You will make great strides in humility by doing this. You will also find great peace.[128]

The spiritual life can be difficult and it is easy to fall into pride (when we fail to realize how little or imperfect we are) or despair (when we consider sanctity to be an impossible task because we do not see yet that it is God who perfects us). Pride and despair are similar in that they eradicate joy. The proud person is self-satisfied but does not possess a joy that is selfless or readily shared with others. The person in despair is miserable, and as self-focused and joyless as the proud.

What a relief it is to realize that our sanctity doesn't depend on our perfection—but on God's perfection in us. And that God cannot perfect us until we hand Him all our sins, failures, and faults—the bad as well as the good. In this way God is able to sanctify us *not in spite of* our faults and failings, but *through and because of* our faults and failings—and, yes, even our sins.

God can transform us through our sin provided we go to Him in humility. Our weaknesses and imperfections are all

---

[127] Andre Frossard, *Forget Not Love: The Passion of Maximilian Kolbe* (San Francisco: Ignatius, 1991), 117.

[128] Note that this "way" is not to be used as a justification or excuse for sin. It is, rather, a way of allowing God to use our inevitable falls and failings as a means of drawing us closer to Him.

we really have that are truly our own and He cannot lift us up into union with Him until we give even these to Him. And we must do this over and over again.

This should give us great hope! To know that all we have to do is go to Him with our falls, messes, and scrapes. That we need only lay them at His feet like a child, tell Him, "I am sorry," and then ask for His help. He is our loving Father and He will not deny us.

I find great comfort in these words of Our Lord to Saint Faustina:

> My daughter, imagine that you are the sovereign of all the world and have the power to dispose of all things according to your good pleasure. You have the power to do all the good you want, and suddenly a little child knocks on your door, all trembling and in tears and, trusting in your kindness, asks for a piece of bread lest he die of starvation. What would you do for this child? Answer Me, my daughter.[129]

Saint Faustina prayed, "sufferings, adversities, humiliations, failures and suspicions that have come my way are splinters that keep alive the fire of my love for You, O Jesus."[130] May you do the same.

READING LIST

+ Graham Greene, *The Power and the Glory* (fiction; the protagonist priest is prepared by God for martyrdom and

---

[129] *Dairy*, no. 229.
[130] Ibid., 57.

sainthood through suffering and various humiliations
occasioned by his significant failings)

+ Evelyn Waugh, *Brideshead Revisited* (fiction; a reflection
on God's grace and mercy in the life of a sinner)

The Magdalene: Healing and Conversion

Dear Marie Therese,

Not every young woman called to religious life has been as well catechized as you or blessed with the loving and stable family life you had.

Some of us were raised in Catholic families but were poorly formed. We didn't receive the spiritual or intellectual formation we needed, and so we don't know our faith the way we should. Some women come to religious life as converts. They have lived in the world, according to the ways of the world, and then found Our Lord and entered into friendship with Him.

Others don't have a life-changing conversion but as cradle or "rocking horse" Catholics[136] must engage in a life-long battle against lukewarmness and mediocrity—moving up towards sanctity, then sliding back down; climbing up, and then falling down again.

Many have also been hurt by divorce, neglect, or abuse. They carry emotional and spiritual scars associated with the widespread breakdown of the family and the sexual revolution. These wounds can lead to a lack of inner freedom—they stop us from loving others and ourselves in ways that are wholesome and free. They stop us from seeing ourselves as we really are—beautiful, beloved daughters of God.

---

[136] This is how the late mystic Caryll Houselander described herself in her autobiography, *A Rocking Horse Catholic*.

Sometimes these wounds will interfere with a woman's ability to enter and live out religious life. The kind, duration, and frequency of the abuse and/or trauma as well as the age of the woman when the abuse occurred will determine the severity of the wounds and the degree to which they negate a religious vocation. A mother superior I greatly admire and respect, explained it to me in this way:

> While God is always victorious and always desires our sanctity, sometimes the residual effects of neglect, abuse, or trauma can actually be an impediment to religious life, as we have found. The type, duration and developmental moment when it occurred in the life of the young woman all determine the impact and the degree to which the trauma has lasting effects ... these may be potential impediments, but it only means that God has something else beautiful planned for the young person discerning!

So while these wounds might prevent a woman from pursuing religious life, they will not stop God from calling her to holiness. God does not restrict Himself to human expectations or measures of respectability. Ignorance, degradation, and trauma—none of these will hold Our Lord back from calling a woman to be a saint. There is simply no accounting for grace.

Saint Mary Magdalene, or the Magdalene as she is sometimes known, had seven demons cast out of her. She is traditionally thought to have been a prostitute. She met Our Lord and became one of the greatest saints in the history of the Church. It was she to whom Our Lord first appeared after His Resurrection.[137]

Saint Margaret of Cortona was a rich man's mistress and had a child out of wedlock. She entered religious life and died a saint.[138]

The children of Fatima didn't know who or what the "Holy Father" was. When they saw a vision of the Pope, they described him simply as "the Bishop dressed in White."[139] While Jacinta and Francisco died young, Lúcia entered religious life and eventually became a Carmelite.

Saint Josephine Bakhita was born in Sudan and abducted from her parents by Arab slave traders at only eight or so years of age.[140] She was made a slave, forced to convert to Islam, and then sold and bought many times over. Some of her owners were cruel and physically abused her.[141] One mutilated her skin with a razor and salt causing over a hundred scars on her torso and right arm.[142] She was freed in Italy and baptized as a Catholic at twenty-one.[143] Three years later, Saint Josephine Bakhita entered religious life. She became a Canossian religious sister and one of the great saints of modern Africa.

Women who come to religious life with a more difficult or unconventional background will, however, have some hurdles to overcome.

---

[137] "St. Mary Magdalen," in *Butler's Lives of the Saints*, 3:161–163.

[138] "St. Margaret of Cortona," Ibid., vol. 1, *January, Februrary, March*, 396–399.

[139] Leo Madigan, *The Children of Fatima: Blessed Francisco & Blessed Jacinta Marto* (Huntington, IN: Our Sunday Visitor, 2003), 135.

[140] Roberto Italo Zanini, *Bakhita: From Slave to Saint* (San Francisco: Ignatius, 2013), 37.

[141] Ibid., 56–57.

[142] Ibid., 59–61.

[143] Ibid., 87–91.

I am told that one of the biggest problems faced by candidates for religious life is a lack of knowledge about the Catholic faith. A priest wrote to say:

> In my pastoral experience, a basic catechesis is lacking in young Catholic people. Most seminaries and religious houses offer basic catechetics to incoming candidates for it simply is not there. There may be a love of the Lord and a recent conversion, but an understanding of virtue, grace, human nature, the teachings of the Church are not there.[144]

This is easily corrected with some diligence. Again, I encourage you to read Leo Trese's introduction to the Catholic faith called *The Faith Explained*. It provides an excellent overview of our beautiful faith.

A second hurdle concerns the emotional and spiritual wounds inflicted by divorce and the sexual revolution. The same priest writes that: "The instability of marriage creates instability of character in children, which leads a lack of inner freedom for many."[145] If this applies to a young woman, she should attempt to heal her wounds before she enters religious life. This is the more difficult task and it will require prayer, humility, and perseverance. As our dear Father V. would put it, she needs to approach this battle on two fronts: the spiritual and the emotional.

---

[144] Fr. Anthony Baetzold to the author, May 17, 2016.
[145] Ibid.

First Front: Spiritual Healing

She should start by entrusting the healing process to Saint Mary Magdalene. She should ask the Magdalene to be her special patron as she addresses the instability and wounds she received during her upbringing or as a young adult in the secular world.

She should ask God to show her what wounds she has. Ask Him to heal them. Ask Him for the grace to cooperate with His healing.

She should receive the Sacrament of Penance and Reconciliation. This is God's preferred method of healing and it is a most precious gift. She should go to Confession on a weekly or fortnightly basis, and she'll receive much grace to overcome her spiritual wounds, venial sins, and involuntary faults.

She should consider attending Eucharistic Adoration on a regular basis and spend time in front of Our Lord in the Blessed Sacrament. She should ask Him during these intimate moments together to heal her.

Women who have struggled with impurity (however bad) and who are called to religious life should pray for perseverance in holy purity but also for a healing of their emotions and imagination. Conversely, women who have lived chastely need to be wary of spiritual pride. This sort of pride is extremely poisonous and will hurt not only your own spiritual development but that of others. Ask God for humility.

Women who have been abused or neglected should pray that God take away the distorted and muddied filters through which they see themselves so that they can appreciate their true worth—their infinite value as children of God.

They should also pray for the gifts of confidence and forgiveness. Women who have been hurt don't always have the confidence to draw appropriate boundaries, be calmly assertive, or insist on having their needs met and respected.

These same women can also struggle with anger. God and His mother will help them overcome these wounds if they ask. Healing won't happen overnight but with grace and persistent effort, they will become the women God has always intended them to be.

Second Front: Emotional Healing

Catholics sometimes resist or belittle therapy. We forget that we are physical and emotional beings as well as spiritual beings. We hope that prayer and the sacraments will suffice. Sometimes they do, but God also wants for us to benefit from the wisdom and gifts of our fellow Christians, and for this reason seeing a good Catholic therapist can be extremely helpful.

Do seek out therapy if there have been difficulties in your life that need attention, discussion, and healing:

> Therapy is aimed at healing and correcting underlying issues that, left untreated, can lead to critical situations. As such it can be most productive when you are *not* in an active crisis. Think of it this way: crises are like active fires that need to be contained and extinguished. But once they are under control, you need to find out what is fueling them so they do not reoccur. If you find your life seems to be a series of crises, bro-

ken relationships, and chaos then therapy can be very beneficial to you.[146]

However, please remember this important proviso: make sure your therapist is a committed Catholic!

While some Catholics refuse to see therapy as a useful tool, others jump right in and are undiscerning about the advice they are given or the therapist they see. Some therapists, psychologists, or psychiatrists do not understand our Catholic faith. At best they see it as dispensable. At worst they view it with hostility and suspicion, and will try to "release" you from the "burden" of your Judeo-Christian beliefs. These therapists do great harm to the Christians and Catholics who stumble into their counsel.

The website CatholicTherapists.com has a useful e-book available free online called *What Every Catholic Should Know Before Starting Therapy*.

READING LIST

Conversions and Difficulties
+ Rumer Godden, *Five for Sorrow, Ten for Joy* (fiction)
+ Graham Greene, *The End of the Affair* (fiction)
+ Caryll Houselander, *A Rocking Horse Catholic*
+ Mother Veronica Namoyo le Goulard, P.C.C., *A Memory for Wonders: A True Story*
+ Evelyn Waugh, *Brideshead Revisited* (fiction)

---

[146] CatholicTherapists.com, *What Every Catholic Should Know* Before *Starting Therapy* (2016), 3, http://www.catholictherapists.com/images/before-starting-therapy.pdf.

Faith Formation

+ Leo J. Trese, *The Faith Explained*

Therapy

+ *What Every Catholic Should Know* Before *Starting Therapy*: http://www.catholictherapists.com/images/before-starting-therapy.pdf
+ Finding a Catholic therapist:
  + www.WellCatholic.com
  + www.CatholicTherapists.com

FEAR OF SUFFERING

Dear Marie Therese,

A significant obstacle to entering religious life and increasing in sanctity is fear of suffering.

Fear of suffering has been significant in my own struggle to grow in sanctity. I love Jesus but I don't always love Him enough to want to suffer for Him in the ways He asks of me.

When I become impatient and lose my temper because I am inconvenienced, it is because I am unwilling to suffer this inconvenience for Him. When I am bothered or disturbed by the poor opinion others have of me, it is because I am unwilling to accept humiliation for Him. When I indulge in sadness because I can't discern what path to take in some matter, it is because I am unwilling to endure blindness for Him. When I allow myself to feel anxious or irritated by the chaos that accompanies living with and raising small children, it is because I am unwilling to practice detachment and suffer a lack of order for Him.

You cannot become a saint and you cannot overcome your imperfections if you are unwilling to suffer. You cannot join Jesus in heaven if you are unwilling to join Him on the Cross beforehand.

Most young women are unwilling to sacrifice marriage and motherhood for God. They cling to their fertility and youth as though these passing things will be with them forever. They do not stay with you! They too will pass! Slowly, slowly—even in a wonderful Christian marriage—you will feel the passing of the years and the toil of parenthood erode your looks and youthful feminine charm.

Others may tell you that your life will be wasted as a religious. These detractors imagine religious life as a dour, joyless confinement in which nothing good is experienced or produced.

All this fear is incongruous with the reality of religious life. My friends who are religious sisters are among the most joyful women I know! They are bright, cheerful, and vibrant. They emanate tremendous joy and serenity—not in spite of, but because of their vows and sacrifices.

As Aurora Griffin astutely notes in her book *How I Stayed Catholic at Harvard*, much of the fear about religious life stems from a misidentification of its challenges:

> The religious men and women I've talked to find great freedom in their vows of poverty, chastity, and obedience. The challenges for consecrated religious often involve spiritual attacks from the enemy—discord in the community, doubt about the existence of God, or a lukewarm prayer life.[147]

On the other hand, she also observes (accurately) that many people underestimate the challenges of marriage:

> In order to make the right decision about your vocation, you must be realistic about the challenges of your options. I feel like a lot of my friends who want

---

[147] Aurora Griffin, *How I Stayed Catholic at Harvard: Forty Tips for Faithful College Students* (San Francisco: Ignatius Press, 2016), 97.

to get married think about all the wonderful parts of planning a wedding and going on a honeymoon and do not seriously consider the sacrifices involved in married life. At its best, marriage offers the consolation of companionship, sex, and security. But marriage also involves incredible self-sacrifice and personal risk. Abuse, infidelity, widowing, and divorce are true threats, not to mention all the contingencies involved with raising children. People are quick to dismiss these realities because they are afraid of being alone.[148]

If you are fearful of suffering, you might find this prayer by Saint Faustina helpful:

Mother of God, Your soul was plunged into a sea of bitterness; look upon Your child and teach her to suffer and to love while suffering. Fortify my soul that pain will not break it. Mother of grace, teach me to live by [the power of] God.[149]

Pray to Our Lady and all the martyrs for the courage you need to enter religious life should this be your calling.

---

[148] Ibid., 97.
[149] *Diary*, no. 315.

EXPIATION

Dear Marie Therese,

Some are held back in sanctity by fear of suffering. Others are undone when they overestimate their ability to bear suffering.

Do not ask for suffering. Do not offer yourself as a victim soul unless this is specifically requested of you and permitted by your confessor. If you do ask, you might not be prepared for what is given.

If you desire to suffer for Jesus, the better option is to become a soul of passive expiation.

What do I mean by this?

God grants the soul many things to suffer throughout the day and from week to week. These sufferings are passive in so far as they are unasked for and not at all sought out. Often they are little. Sometimes they are significant.

Take these unasked-for sufferings and offer them back to Jesus in atonement for your sins and the sins of others.

Let me give you some examples:

+ When you experience a toothache, seek the help and medical care you need, but in the meantime offer the pain to Jesus in expiation for your or others' sins of gluttony, detraction, idle chatter, or blasphemy.
+ When you are made to wait (in a checkout line at the supermarket, at the bank, in the car waiting for your mother to finish her conversation with someone, etc.)

offer this suffering to Jesus in expiation for the times you've lacked patience or when you've been inconsiderate of others' time.

+ When you're unable to get your hair cut or buy a dress or a pair of shoes that you'd like, offer this up to Our Lord in reparation for your sins of vanity, or for when you or others have been wasteful with money.

+ When you experience pain associated with your monthly cycle, offer this up in atonement for the ongoing sin and horror of abortion.

And so on.

This hidden, humble way of expiation lacks the presumption and pride involved when one asks for suffering. Best of all, when done cheerfully and discretely, it is pleasing to Our Lord.

Ask the Holy Spirit for light. Ask Him to show you how to do this and for which sins He'd like you to atone. Do not ask for suffering but for enlightenment. Ask for the Holy Spirit to be in your soul like a flame in a lantern, for when God illuminates, He also eviscerates. When you let Him in, His light both reveals and removes sin. Ask Him to burn in you and to incinerate all that keeps you from Him.

❧

Evangelization through Love

Dear Marie Therese,

The other day we discussed a conversation that took place in which Our Lord's name was disrespected. You were very hard on yourself for not speaking up and correcting the person at fault. Perhaps you should have, but it is also possible that you did the right thing in saying nothing.

If the correction could not be given lovingly or without publicly shaming the person, perhaps you were right not to offer it. Speaking up would have done justice to God but it would not have been loving to that soul or helpful in turning it towards God. The more perfect way might have been to remain silent and to praise God's name internally—to make an act of contrition and mortification for that soul so that it receives the grace it needs to reform.

God loves that soul and wants her to love and know Him.

Severity is often a necessary part of mercy. But correction must come from a person who has the authority to give it. And even then it must be sourced in love for the other and not from love of self or indignant self-satisfaction. We must always try to live out and reflect God's love for the souls of others.

Consider the example of Blessed Pier Giorgio Frassati. When his parents fell away from the faith, he would come to the dinner table last and make the sign of the cross just before entering the room.[150] He paused to say grace. By privately thanking God for the meal he was about to enjoy, he

---

[150] Luciana Frassati, *A Man of the Beatitudes*, 44.

was able to give God His due but avoided shaming his parents or parading his faith in front of them. Blessed Pier Giorgio joyfully accepted death, asking God for the preservation of his parents' crumbling marriage and their conversion.[151] His love for them was in conformity with the way of perfection. It was evangelization through love.

This evangelization through love does not mean being soft or denying Christ's words or teachings, or the teachings of the Catholic Church. There is a tendency today to want a one-size-fits-all approach to evangelization. More worrying, the need for a "New Evangelization" seems to have been misunderstood, or rather, misappropriated by those who would like the Church to change in praxis, if not doctrine. Their thinking is that more people will come to know and love Jesus if the Catholic Church is less precise, less orthodox, less doctrinal—less black-and-white on moral issues. This "take" on the New Evangelization is shortsighted and—as the mainline Protestant churches have already shown—will not succeed.

Let us be clear on what the New Evangelization is and is not. The New Evangelization does not mean going to the peripheries and staying there. It does not mean changing the faith to make it more palatable to the world! Rather, it is the re-evangelization of fallen away Catholics and the re-evangelization of our increasingly pagan culture. It is the proclamation of Christ to all peoples—including those already within the folds of the Church.[152]

---

[151] Ibid., 148.

[152] John Paul II, "The Task of the Latin American bishops," *Origins* 12 (March 24, 1983). Properly speaking, of course, "evangelization cannot be new in its content since its very theme is always the one gospel given in Jesus Christ" (Ibid., 659–662).

True evangelization is done by God and occurs only with prayer, and through a loving personal relationship between our soul and that of another, and then that soul and God. Every Christian is called to evangelize, but *how* we evangelize depends upon (a) who we are and our state of life, and (b) who we are evangelizing. Our most important and effective evangelization occurs when we lead a life of prayer and try to fulfill our duties of state as joyfully, humbly, and lovingly as we can.

The French mystic Elisabeth Leseur provides us with a lived example of this. Elisabeth was married to an ardent atheist who sought to destroy her faith. Despite the hostility of those she loved and the spiritual isolation she felt, Elisabeth returned to the faith after a brief lapse and became very holy. She fulfilled "superbly the obligations of her state"[153] and engaged in an intellectual apostolate to bring Christ to the "politicians, publicists, journalists, physicians, university men, scholars, men of letters, musicians, playwrights, and artists"[154] they ordinarily associated with. She did this by resolving:

> To *give* to others serenity, charm, kindness, useful words and deeds. To make Christian truth loved through me, but to speak of it only at an explicit demand or at a need so clear as to seem truly providential. To preach by prayer, sacrifice, and example. To be *austere* to myself, and as *attractive* as possible to others.[155]

---

[153] Elisabeth Leseur, *The Secret Diary of Elisabeth Leseur*, xviii.

[154] Ibid., xxiv.

[155] Ibid., 63. Emphasis in original.

Like Blessed Pier Giorgio, Elisabeth died a victim soul, having offered her life for the conversion and salvation of her husband, Felix.[156]

Your main method of evangelization as a student living a pre-vocational life will be to fulfill, as lovingly as possible, your duties as a Catholic daughter and student. Humbly and joyfully live out and fulfill your duties of state. People will—over time—notice the joy, hard work, and integrity with which you carry this out. In going about your life this way, you'll also be given opportunities to witness to others and develop friendships with them. By loving and praying for these souls—seeking out always what is best for them—you will win hearts and minds for Christ.

Remember too that your part-time work as a nanny for our family and other families like ours (as well as the assistance and love you give to your brothers and sisters) is also an important work of evangelization. The home and family are the first frontier of evangelization.

Christians cannot live in isolation. Your faith will not survive outside of a Christian community or family (unless you have a specific calling to eremitic life). Serving our family in the way that you do adds to and builds up our local Christian community. The dedication, diligence, and love you show to me and my children day after day, week after week, and month after month is a reflection of God's own devotion and love for us, and it strengthens me in my state of life as a wife and mother.

---

[156] Ibid., xiii and xxv. After Elisabeth's death, Felix converted to the Catholic faith and became a priest. He entered the Dominican Order and became a "Black Friar." Elisabeth's confessor and spiritual director considered Elisabeth to be a saint, and I have no doubt that she will one day by recognized as such by the Church.

Remember no one is saved until he is dead and in purgatory or heaven. No one is a saint or assured of heaven until then. Unfortunately, many in the Church seem to have forgotten this. Some bishops, priests, religious, and lay members of the Church are keen to tend to those at the periphery but fail to meet the needs of those already in the Church.

The parable of the good shepherd in Matthew (18:12–14) and Luke (15:3–7) is often given as a justification for this. The parable in Matthew is as follows:

> If a man has a hundred sheep, and one of them has gone astray. Does not he leave the ninety-nine on the hills and go in search of the one that went astray? And if he finds it, truly, I say to you, he rejoices over it more than over the ninety-nine that never went astray.

The wording in Luke is similar:

> So he told them this parable: "What man of you, having a hundred sheep, if he has lost one of them, does not leave the ninety-nine in the wilderness, and go after the one which is lost, until he finds it? And when he has found it, he lays it on his shoulders, rejoicing. And when he comes home, he calls together his friends and his neighbors, saying to them "Rejoice with me, for I have found my sheep which was lost." Just so, I tell you, there will be more joy in heaven over one sinner who repents than over ninety-nine righteous persons who need no repentance.

This parable is often cited in support of focusing missionary efforts almost exclusively on those outside or at the margins of the Church. This is a thin reading of the parable and it fails to take into account the words of John 10:

> I am the good shepherd. The good shepherd lays down his life for the sheep. He who is a hireling and not a shepherd, whose own the sheep are not, sees the wolf coming and leaves the sheep and flees; and the wolf snatches them and scatters them. He flees because he is a hireling and cares nothing for the sheep. I am the good shepherd; I know my own and my own know me, as the Father knows me and I know the Father; and I lay down my life for the sheep. And I have other sheep that are not of this fold; I must bring them also, and they will heed my voice. So there shall be one flock, one shepherd. (Jn 10:11–16)

Yes, the shepherd leaves his flock to rescue the one stray sheep. But he does not leave his flock unfed or unsafe. The good shepherd should make sure the ninety-nine are safely enclosed and have the warmth, space, food, shade, light, and water they need before heading off to reclaim the lost one. The parable as told in Luke and Matthew assumes that there will be an intact flock for the one lost sheep to join when found. What sort of victory would it be to reclaim one lost sheep if the other ninety-nine were lost in the process?

Read in conjunction with John 10, we must understand that the shepherd cares for and loves his flock just as he loves the lost sheep, and that he wants the lost sheep to be part of the one, unified fold.

Often priests or laypeople engaged in apostolates that cater to the faithful are told that they are just "preaching to the choir." The subtext, of course, is "why bother?" And yet, if bishops, priests and religious fail to tend to the "choir" and meet its needs, the flock will be decimated.

Imagine locking the "choir" in a closet or prison without air, sunlight, food, or water. The members of this worthy little choir wouldn't last long. The choir needs water. They need food—in short, they need spiritual sustenance. They need access to sound preaching and liturgy free of abuse. Similarly, their children require authentic Catholic schools where sound intellectual and spiritual formation is imparted by faithful, practicing Catholics. As the last fifty years have shown, when the choir is denied its basic spiritual needs, it dwindles in size and vitality.

In other words, when we do find the lost sheep and bring them home, there won't be a fold for the lost sheep to belong to.

For examples of great modern-day evangelists, laypersons living a pre-vocation life should look to Blessed Pier Giorgio Frassati and Saint Teresa of the Andes for instruction on charity and evangelization.[157] Parents should look to Saints Louis and Zélie Martin, and the saintly father of Saint John Paul II (also named Karol Wojtyła).[158] Wives and women in

---

[157] Luciana Frassati, *A Man of the Beatitudes*; Jennifer Moorcroft, *God is All Joy*; and Saint Teresa of the Andes, *Letters*.

[158] See Stephane-Joseph Piat, *The Story of a Family: The Home of St. Thérèse of Lisieux* (Charlotte, NC: TAN Books, 1994); and George Weigel, *Witness to Hope: The Biography of Pope John Paul II* (New York: Harper, 1999).

the world should model Elisabeth Leseur.[159] Husbands look to Dietrich von Hildebrand.[160] Religious sisters should rely on Saint Thérèse of Lisieux.[161] Parish priests should turn to Saint John Vianney.[162]

Ask Blessed Pier Giorgio Frassati to intercede on your behalf and teach you to evangelize through love.

---

[159] Elisabeth Leseur, *The Secret Diary of Elisabeth Leseur*. See also Alice von Hildebrand, *By Love Refined: Letters to a Young Bride* (Manchester, NH: Sophia Institute, 1989).

[160] Alice von Hildebrand, *The Soul of a Lion: The Life of Dietrich von Hildebrand* (San Francisco: Ignatius, 2000), 144. After Dietrich became a Catholic, every single one of his siblings and all but one of their spouses followed him into the Church (one sister converted prior to Dietrich). All his nephews and nieces were raised Catholic.

[161] See Saint Teresa of Jesus of the Andes, *Letters of Saint Teresa of Jesus of the Andes*, and Saint Thérèse of Lisieux, *Story of a Soul*.

[162] George W. Rutler, *The Cure D'Ars Today: St. John Vianney* (San Francisco: Ignatius, 1988).

ASKING FOR SIGNS

Dear Marie Therese,

You might be tempted to ask God to give you a specific sign as to whether or not you should enter the convent. Don't. Although shortcuts like this are appealing, you are testing God and opening yourself up to deception and disappointment.

God has already given us ordinary means of obtaining grace and an ordinary means of discernment—means such as the sacraments which are, in and of themselves, great mysteries and much more awesome to behold and ponder than any sign we might come up with.

It is always possible, of course, that God will give you a sign or push you in one direction or the other, but do not ask for or expect this. Be grateful if it is given, but don't seek it out.

Some Practical Matters

Dear Marie Therese,

In preparing for marriage, there are said to be three preparatory stages:

1. remote stage,
2. proximate stage, and
3. immediate stage.[164]

The remote stage of preparation is the early formation and education of a soul, primarily by her parents. The proximate stage refers to the engagement period in which a couple prepares for marriage by deepening their faith life, reading and learning about marriage, and receiving moral and theological formation. The Church also uses this period to assess whether the candidates meet the psychological, legal, and medical requirements for marriage within the Catholic Church. In the immediate stage, the couple tends to all the ecclesiastical and material steps necessary for marriage.

The first two stages (remote and proximate) have their analogous counterparts in preparation for religious life.

I won't write anything on the remote stage here but would like to address some issues that will arise as you enter more deeply into the proximate stage of preparation.

---

[164] Pontifical Council for the Family, *Preparation for the Sacrament of Marriage* (1996), http://www.vatican.va/roman_curia/pontifical_councils/family/documents/rc_pc_family_doc_13051996_preparation-for-marriage_en.html.

Debt

One requirement for entry into religious life is that the candidate be debt free.

You have done well to avoid college debt. Continue to be frugal and self-disciplined in how you spend your money. Live within your means and—whatever you do—do not go into debt.[165]

The allure of travel and having "experiences" is often difficult for college students to resist. This is fine if you have the funds to pay for a trip in full.[166] However, if you do not have a sufficient sum saved up, then resist the urge to take expensive trips or buy expensive items.

An aside: it's a mistake to assume that entering a religious order will mean you will never travel again. The semi-active orders often send their religious here and there on mission trips or pilgrimages. In fact, the sisters I know who have joined semi-active orders travel more than many wives and mothers I know. Marriage comes with obligations and responsibilities—to your spouse and his work, to children and their health and educational needs, and to your own and your spouse's extended family. Do not assume that marriage and family will afford you more freedom. This is not always the case.

Investigate

Take time to investigate and learn about religious life. Right now your knowledge is mostly theoretical. You need to understand the basic differences between the enclosed and semi-active orders, and you should start to develop a sense

---

[165] This includes credit card debt.
[166] Assuming the travel is appropriate.

for the different charisms of the various orders open to you.

What is a charism? The charism of a religious order is the particular way in which its members are called to love and serve God. It is given by God to the order as a gift for the benefit of the entire Church, and is what gives the order its particular character or orientation:

> A charism—says St. Paul—is a particular "manifestation of the Spirit given to each one *for the common good*" (1 Cor 12:7). St. Peter says the same thing when he writes "to the extent that each of you has received a gift (*charisma*), use it to serve one another as good stewards of God's varied grace" (cf. 1 Peter 4:10).[167]

The Dominicans are called, for example, to contemplate God and to give to others the fruits of their contemplation. It is for this reason that they are known as the Order of Preachers. The Franciscans are called to live out the Gospel of Our Lord Jesus Christ in a particular way and to proclaim the Gospel to others. The Sisters of Life take a fourth vow to protect and enhance the sacredness of human life. Their unique charism flows from this and expresses itself through their work and prayers as a reverence and gratitude for the unique and unrepeatable gift of each and every human life.

To begin your understanding of religious life, start by reading a delightful book entitled, *A Few Lines to Tell You: My Life in Carmel* by Sister Marie, O.C.D. It is difficult to

---

[167] Raniero Cantalamessa, O.F.M. Cap., *Virginity: A Positive Approach to Celibacy for the Sake of the Kingdom of Heaven* (Staten Island, NY: St. Pauls, 1995), 63.

find in paperback form but a digital copy can be obtained for free from the online HathiTrust Digital Library. More readily available is the book, *A Right to Be Merry* by Mother Mary Francis, P.C.C., which describes life in a Poor Clare cloister. *Barefoot Journey* by Sister Felicity P.C.C. is also about the Poor Clares.

In This House of Brede by Rumer Godden should be available through your library system, and provides a delightful, fictional account of life in an enclosed Benedictine priory. The first few chapters of *The Deliverance of Sister Cecilia* by William Brinkley describe the life of a sister upon entering a semi-active religious order. This book is an easy, edifying read.

My advice to you—I cannot press this upon you enough—is to spend a week with a contemplative order and a week with a semi-active order as soon as you can.

You might be surprised by what appeals to you and what doesn't. I had assumed God wanted me to become a Dominican and would never have thought to join an enclosed, contemplative order. However, after spending time at the Tyburn priory in Australia and the Tyburn convent in London, I longed to become a Tyburn nun. It was to this order that I was drafting a letter for permission to enter when God made me understand that He did not want me to enter at all.

Ask Saint Faustina to intercede for you in finding the right order. After she entered the Sisters of Our Lady of Mercy, she decided to leave so she could enter an enclosed, contemplative order. She wanted more time to devote to prayer than what was possible with the Sisters of Our Lady of Mercy (a semi-active community). Our Lord appeared to her with open wounds on His face and crying large tears. He rebuked her for this decision saying: "It is you who will cause Me this pain if you leave this convent. It is to this place that I called you and nowhere else; and I have prepared many graces for you."[168] Don't be preemptive by closing any doors to Jesus. Let Jesus close and open them for you.

Some Additional Considerations

When considering which religious order to join, look for orders that are vibrant and joyful and which strive to be faithful, not only to the Church and its traditions and teachings, but also to the Rule and traditions of their own order and founder.[169] Attempting to join an order in decline with the intention of reform is likely to lead to frustration and a possible loss of vocation.

Some women might toy with the idea of starting a new order. Try to keep in mind that very few souls are called to found orders and many of them receive this calling only after they have entered religious life.[170] God will make it clear if you are called to begin something new. Until He does, assume that you are not and that you need to find an established order to join.

Impediments

Certain physical, mental, or emotional disabilities may prevent you from entering religious life.

---

168 *Diary*, no. 19.

169 For young women residing in the United States, I suggest looking into an order affiliated with the Council of Major Superiors of Women Religious before considering those associated with the Leadership Conference of Women Religious.

170 The most recent saintly example being Mother Teresa. She was called to found the Missionaries of Charity only after she was a Loreto sister.

To enter a particular order, you need to be capable of doing all that is demanded of the sisters in that order. If you have a physical, a mental, or an emotional handicap that will prevent you from fulfilling your duties of state, then you probably don't have a vocation to that order—if at all.

Abbott William, founder of the Maronite Monks of Adoration, began his religious life as a Trappist. Because of his undiagnosed hypoglycemia, he was unable to fulfill the austere demands of the Trappist life at that time. It took Abbott William many years before he was able to discern where God wanted him to live out his religious vocation. The Abbott's patient trust in God during this long period of uncertainty was remarkable.

One of the most common impediments I have seen in young women desiring the religious life is depression. If you have or are struggling with clinical depression, you will likely be refused entry. The same goes for bipolar disorder, schizophrenia, and all the various personality disorders.

If you find yourself in this position, do not be ashamed or feel humiliated. It is hard not to feel rejected, but ask God for the grace to love your cross.

Caryll Houselander, a "divine eccentric" who lived in England during the last century, struggled with what she termed "neurosis" but argued—I believe correctly—that "neurosis" or mental and emotional difficulties can be a means of achieving great sanctity. This particular cross, with all its sorrow, mental anguish, lack of emotional control, humiliation, judgment, and exclusion, can be a path to sanctity when united to Jesus' suffering on the Cross and in the Garden of Gethsemane. You might not become a religious sister, but you can still become a saint.

Exceptions

There are, of course, exceptions to some impediments. Sometimes an order—because of its charism—can accept women with particular needs.

There is an order in France, the Institute of the Little Sisters Disciples of the Lamb, where young women with Down's syndrome can enter religious life. Also of French origin are the Dominican Sisters of Bethany, who work with incarcerated women and sometimes welcome formerly imprisoned women into their order as religious sisters. The Order of the Visitation of the Virgin Mary was founded by Saint Francis de Sales and Saint Jane Frances de Chantal "as a haven for those whose health, age or other considerations debarred them from the already established orders."[171]

Keep in mind, however, that in the spiritual life, we should almost always abide by the ordinary means or ways of doing things established for us by Jesus and His Church. God allows for exceptions, but you should assume that you are not an exception—that you are called to do things as they are usually done. If you are to take an alternative route—if you are to be an exception to the norm—God will make it very clear. Until He does, assume that the usual rules, norms, and ways of doing things apply to you.

Homesickness

Entering religious life will bring a number of upheavals for you and your family. One such upheaval is that you will have to leave your home, and possibly your city and country, to enter the convent God has chosen for you. When you do, I

---

[171] "St. Jane Frances de Chantal," in *Butler's Lives of the Saints*, 3:371.

imagine that you will miss your family, home, and friends.

It is a way of life for military families to move every few years. Some semi-active religious orders also periodically re-assign their members. Even in a contemplative community you might be asked after a time to migrate to a different state, country, or continent to assist in the founding of a new convent or priory.

It helps to remember that there is no permanent place for us here on earth. Heaven is our true home.

As you prepare to enter religious life, meditate on Our Lady's flight into Egypt with Joseph and baby Jesus. Mary didn't have much warning. God, through His angel, instructed Joseph to flee with his family. Joseph was immediately obedient to God, and Mary, in turn, was immediately obedient to Joseph. In Egypt they had no family, friends, home, or livelihood. The language, culture, and religion of this place were foreign to them. We can imagine how much they might have missed their life in Nazareth.

Ask our Lady of Exile to aid and accompany you.

Parental and Sibling Grief

You are aware that your parents and siblings may grieve your absence when you enter religious life. They will miss you just as you miss them. Begin to pray for them now, before you enter.

Ask God to take care of them. Ask God to give them the grace to accept this loss in a holy way. Entrust them to Saint Anne and Saint Joachim who were separated from their daughter Mary more than once as Mary followed God's call and fulfilled His will.

It is generally agreed that Mary and Joseph spent two to five years with Jesus in Egypt and that Saint Anne was not with them—at least, not initially. Tradition also has it that Mary spent much of her childhood in the temple, apart from her parents. Saint Anne and Saint Joachim understand the loss, longing, grief, and relinquishment that God is asking of your mother and father.[172] Entrust your mom and dad to Saints Anne and Joachim.

Also, ask Saint Teresa of the Andes to intercede on behalf of your brothers and sisters. Her younger sister, Rebecca, suffered immensely when Saint Teresa became a Carmelite. Eventually Rebecca came to see her sister's entry into Carmel as a gift rather than a loss, later becoming a Carmelite herself.

Saint Teresa of the Andes wrote to Rebecca on Rebecca's fourteenth birthday to tell her that they would be separated:

Believe me, Rebecca, at 14 or 15 people understand their vocation. You hear a voice and a light shows you the path of your life.

That beacon began for me when I turned fourteen. I changed my course and planned the path that I was to follow, and today I am here to share with you my secrets and the dreams and projects I've forged.

Till today the same star has been shining on us

---

[172] Do not, however, let your parents' future grief deter you from entering. Note, however, that I make this statement assuming that one *is* called by God to enter religious life. I leave aside situations where a daughter's entry would cause considerable hardship to her parents or younger siblings. A young woman who wishes to enter religious life but who is also the sole guardian of her younger sisters and brothers might not be able to enter immediately (or at all) if, for example, her entry would mean poverty, instability, separation, or foster care for her siblings.

both. But tomorrow perhaps we won't be together under its protective shadow. This star is our home, it's the family. But we must separate and our hearts, which have been formed in the same way will perhaps not be together tomorrow. Yesterday it seemed to me that you wouldn't understand my explanations but today you're fourteen, the age at which you can understand me. So I believe you'll put yourself in my place and agree with me.

I'll share with you in a few words the secret of my life. Very soon we'll be taken from one another, and the desire we always cherished in our childhood of always living together will quickly be shattered by another higher ideal of our youth. We are to follow different paths in life. To me has been given the better part, as it was given to Magdalene. The Divine Master has taken pity on me. Drawing close to me, He has said to me secretly: "Leave your father and mother and all that you possess and follow Me."

. . . Your sisterly heart must break when you hear me speak of separation, when you hear me murmur that word: goodbye forever on earth that I may imprison myself in Carmel. But, don't be afraid, my dear little sister. There will never be any separation between our souls. I will live in Him. Search for Jesus and in Him you'll find me; and there the three of us will continue our intimate conversations, the lines we'll be carrying on there forever in eternity. How happy I am![173]

---

[173] Teresa of Jesus to Her Sister Rebecca, 15 April 1916, in *Letters*, 10–11.

I can attest from personal experience that Saint Teresa is right. When one of my dearest friends entered Tyburn and shut herself off from the world as a contemplative nun, our friendship did not evaporate but deepened. I drew closer to her following her entry into contemplative life than when I saw her every day.

If you feel that you can, perhaps ask your parents to pray for you. Might they be willing to offer up this separation so that you persevere in faith, purity, and vocation?

Parental Resistance

While your parents can counsel and advise you for or against religious life, they may not keep you from entering the convent. It is outside the scope of their moral and parental authority to do so.[174]

Of course, they may not force or unduly pressure you to enter either! These days the former, rather than the latter, is more common.[175]

---

[174] See CCC 2230. Parents are also restricted from forcing you to marry. Likewise, they cannot prevent you from getting married once you are of age.

[175] A survey conducted by Georgetown University's Center for Applied Research in the Apostolate titled *The Profession Class of 2010: Survey of Women Religious Professing Perpetual Vows: A Report to the Secretariat of Clergy, Consecrated Life & Vocations United States Conference of Catholic Bishops* found that more than half the women making final profession in 2010 were actively discouraged by their parents or family members from entering. Only 26 percent had a mother who encouraged them and a mere 16 percent had a father who was supportive (http://www.usccb.org/beliefs-and-teachings/vocations/consecrated-life/profession-class/upload/profession-class-2010-report.pdf).

Pilgrimages and Mission Trips

There is a popular maxim in the spiritual life that God is never outdone in generosity.[176] It is not uncommon, therefore, to hear that a particular priest discovered his vocation while attending World Youth Day or that a young woman was confirmed in her decision to enter religious life after a pilgrimage to Rome, the Holy Land, or a Marian shrine.

If you are having trouble discerning or feel trepidation about entering religious life, consider going on pilgrimage to a shrine of Our Lady or some other holy place to ask Mary and the saints to intercede on your behalf.

You don't need to travel far to make a pilgrimage. If a longer trip isn't possible, look for shrines and holy places near you, or within easy travel distance. Most major cities house shrines dedicated to Our Lady or a particular saint.

You might also consider setting aside a few months, or perhaps even a year, to do mission work: serving the needs of others by engaging in spiritual and/or corporal works of mercy. The Missionaries of Charity invite volunteers to work with them in India. Closer to home, FOCUS (Fellowship of Catholic University Students) trains college graduates to serve as missionaries on college campuses across the United States.

Doing mission work might also help you discern what charism you are called to as a religious and it will take you out of your everyday routine, thus freeing you to enter religious life more readily.

---

[176] See 2 Corinthians 9:6–15.

READING LIST

Debt Avoidance

+ Dave Ramsey, *The Total Money Makeover: A Proven Plan for Financial Fitness*

Investigate

+ William Brinkley, *The Deliverance of Sister Cecilia* (fiction)
+ Sister Felicity, P.C.C., *Barefoot Journey*
+ Mother Mary Francis, P.C.C., *A Right to Be Merry*
+ Sister Marie, O.C.D., *A Few Lines to Tell You: My Life in Carmel*
+ Rumer Godden, *In This House of Brede* (fiction)
+ James B. Simpson, *Veil and Cowl: Writings from the World of Monks and Nuns*

Impediments

General

+ Abbott William, *A Calling: An Autobiography and the Founding of the Maronite Monks of Adoration*

Depression

+ Aaron Kheriaty and John Cihak, *Catholic Guide to Depression*
+ Saint Thomas More, *The Sadness of Christ*

Exceptions

+ Rumer Godden, *Five for Sorrow, Ten for Joy* (fiction)

Homesickness

+ Franz William, *Mary the Mother of Jesus*, Part III: "The Flight into Egypt" and "The Sojourn in Egypt"
+ Maria von Trapp, *Yesterday, Today and Forever*, Chapter 9: "The Fugitive"

For Parents

+ Brett Brannen, *A Priest in the Family: A Guide for Parents Whose Sons Are Considering Priesthood*
+ Congregation for the Clergy, *Eucharistic Adoration for the Sanctification of Priests and Spiritual Motherhood* (https://www.ewtn.com/library/CURIA/ccladoration.pdf)
+ *For Love Alone: The Story of Women Religious* (2015 documentary by Grassroots Films)
+ Sister Marie, O.C.D., *A Few Lines to Tell You: My Life in Carmel*
+ *The Nun: The Story of a Carmelite Vocation* (2010 documentary by Maud Nycander)

For Younger Siblings, Nieces, and Nephews
Vocation

+ Claire Brandenburg, *The Monk Who Grew Prayer* (3 to 8 years old; introduction to the monastic life)
+ Bryn J. Brock and Karin A. Childs, *The Story of the Call of Samuel* (3 to 7 years; the vocational call of God)
+ *Catholic Children's Treasure Box Books* (2 to 5 years; the chapters on Wupsy and Sunny, and St. Thérèse Lisieux)
+ Nan Gurley, *Little Rose of Sharon: A Story of Self-Sacrifice* (3 to 7 years; religious vocation as a gift of self for others)

+ Sister Marie, O.C.D., *A Few Lines to Tell You: My Life in Carmel* (13 years and up)
+ Josephine Nobisso, *The Weight of a Mass* (4 to 9 years; tale about how the gift of self in vocation mirrors the gift of Jesus in the Blessed Sacrament)
+ Jean Schoonover-Egolf, *Molly McBride and the Purple Habit* (5 to 8 years)
+ Annemarie Thimons, *What is a Vocation?* (4 to 9 years)

More on Monastic Life

+ Katy Beebe, *Brother Hugo and the Bear* (4 to 9 years)
+ Jan Cheripko, *Brother Bartholomew and the Apple Grove* (4 to 8 years)
+ Donna Farley, *The Ravens of Farne: A Tale of Saint Cuthbert* (4 to 8 years)
+ Charlotte Grossetête, *Mother Teresa: The Smile of Calcutta* (4 to 8 years)
+ Dessi Jackson, *Nikola and the Monk* (4 to 8 years)
+ Dessi Jackson, *The Saint and His Bees* (4 to 9 years; Saint Modomnoc, a monk)
+ Marybeth Lorbiecki, *Sister Anne's Hands* (7 to 10 years; about a teaching sister and the beauty of witness to children)
+ Kathleen Norris, *The Holy Twins: Benedict and Scholastica* (4 to 9 years)
+ Jan Pancheri, *Brother William's Year: A Monk at Westminster Abbey* (4 to 8 years)
+ Tomie dePaola, *Pascual and the Kitchen Angels* (3 to 7 years)

+ M. Raymond, *The Family that Overtook Christ: The Amazing Story of the Family of Bernard of Clairvaux* (13 to 18 years)
+ Zélie Redmond, *The Adventures of Sister Regina Marie—Sister Finds a Friend* (5 to 8 years)
+ Jenny Schroedel, *The Blackbird's Nest: Saint Kevin of Ireland* (4 to 8 years)
+ Ann Tompert, *The Pied Piper of Peru* (2 to 8 years)
+ Guido Visconti, *Clare and Francis* (5 to 10 years)
+ Various books about saints and founders published by Vision Books (7 to 12 years)
+ Susan Helen Wallace, *Call Me Little Theresa: St. Theresa of the Child Jesus* (10 years and up)
+ Various books about saints and founders written by Mary Fabyan Windeatt published by TAN books (7 to 12 years)

Martyrdom

Dear Marie Therese,

   We've discussed how you have come to know and love the Traditional Latin Mass. You need to think and pray about how big a sacrifice it will be for you to enter an order where you have limited or no access to Mass in the extraordinary form.

   If that would be a significant cross—one which will challenge your faith or lead to significant difficulties—then you have two options:

1. find a community where the *usus antiquior* is offered either exclusively or with some frequency; or,
2. approach denial of the traditional Mass in the same way you would martyrdom.

Martyrdoms can be of two types: red or white. Red martyrdom is a physical martyrdom. It is called "red" because it is associated with the loss of life (blood). A white martyrdom occurs when a soul accepts great suffering out of love for Jesus. In a white martyrdom, the soul becomes a victim soul. The person does not experience a physical death but undergoes an interior death to self (self-love, self-preservation, and self-preference). It is called "white" because it is a bloodless sacrifice.

   Saint Thomas More explains that martyrdom should be accepted only when God gives you no other option—that martyrdom is not to be voluntarily sought out, but humbly accepted. Why? Because you can't assume you'll have the strength and virtue to faithfully endure the martyrdom:

> Whereto I answered, as the truth is, that I have not been a man of such holy living as I might be bold to offer myself to death, lest God for my presumption might suffer me to fall, and therefore I put not myself forward, but draw back. Howbeit if God draw me to it Himself, then I trust in His great mercy, that He shall not fail to give me grace and strength.[177]

Discuss this with and be guided by your confessor.[178]

READING LIST

The Traditional Mass

+ Pope Benedict XVI, *Summorum Pontificum*
+ Thomas Crean, *The Mass and the Saints*
+ Aurora Griffin, *How I Stayed Catholic at Harvard*, Chapter 21: "Attend a Traditional Mass"
+ Dom Prosper Guéranger, *On the Holy Mass*

---

[177] Thomas Edward Bridgett, *Life and Writings of Blessed Thomas More: Lord Chancellor of England and Martyr Under Henry VIII* (London: Burns, Oates, & Washbourne, 1924), 169.

[178] As a traditional Catholic, it is beneficial (although not necessary) for your confessor to have an appreciation for the Mass in the extraordinary form. What you need to beware of is animus. A priest who is significantly prejudiced against the traditional Mass (despite its legitimacy) will not be able to guide you properly. Similarly, if you have a genuine interest in a community in which the Traditional Latin Mass is largely unavailable, you will need a priest who bears no ill will towards the ordinary form of the Mass (novus ordo Missae).

+ Fr. Francis Randolph, *Know Him in the Breaking of the Bread: A Guide to the Mass*
+ Evelyn Waugh, *A Bitter Trial: Evelyn Waugh and John Cardinal Heenan on the Liturgical Changes*

Red Martyrdom

+ Thomas More, *The Sadness of Christ*
+ Gerard B. Wegemer, *Thomas More: A Portrait of Courage*
+ Evelyn Waugh, *Edmund Campion: A Life*
+ Wilfred Parsons, *Mexican Martyrdom: Firsthand Accounts of the Religious Persecution in Mexico 1926–1935*
+ Waltraud Herbstrith, *Edith Stein: The Untold Story of the Philosopher and Mystic Who Lost Her Life in the Death Camps of Auschwitz*

White Martyrdom

+ Abbot William, *A Calling: An Autobiography and the Founding the Maronite Monks of Adoration*
+ Venerable Fr. Germanus, C.P., *The Life of St. Gemma Galgani*
+ Abbe Francois Trochu, *Saint Bernadette Soubirous 1844–1879*

EXPECTATIONS

Dear Marie Therese,

You need to be aware of the expectations you carry with you when you enter religious life.

As a religious you marry Christ, and while your spouse is perfect (He really *is* the perfect spouse!), the family He gives you is not.

Religious communities—like Catholic families—are microcosms of the Church, made up of fallen, broken people, some of whom will love you very poorly and, from time to time, will (intentionally or inadvertently) cause you great sorrow, pain, and frustration.

When this happens it is easy to become disillusioned. When you first enter into your state of life, the temptation is to idealize your new situation and companions. In marriage, it is not uncommon for a wife to pin all her hopes on her husband. She expects him to make her happy, to provide her with joy and stability. When he fails to live up to her unreasonable expectations (as he inevitably will), she is at risk of falling into anger, melancholy, or despair.

I learned that I could weather the demands and trials of marriage only if I rooted my identity and needs entirely in Christ. Only if Jesus is my rock—only if I seek to have my needs met entirely by Him—will I be free to die to myself here on earth so that I might love and serve others more fully.

Religious need to approach their vocations and religious families in the same way. God will place you in a particular religious community or family, but you must root your identity and hopes firmly in Him. You must look to Jesus to satiate you. You must look to Him, rather than your community, to be your ultimate source of fulfillment and security.

Yes, you will love Jesus by loving the sisters He gives you in community, but you will be able to do this fully and joyfully only if you anchor yourself first in Jesus. Do not expect your fellow sisters to satisfy you. They cannot fulfill your desires. They cannot provide you with the full measure of joy, calm, stability, and security you desire. If you expect this of them, you are sure to be disappointed.

Only by anchoring yourself entirely in God will you be able to love your fellow sisters in the way they deserve to be loved by you. Paradoxically, the more you forget yourself and your own needs, the happier you'll be. The less you think of yourself and your happiness, the more joy you'll eventually come to have and give to others.

You can only do this by loving Christ above all things—by putting Him first in your heart. He needs to be the one you turn to first to fulfill your desires, hopes, and needs.

When suffering and trials come—whether in marriage or religious life—you can only undergo the pain that accompanies growth in sanctity by putting God first. This allows you to welcome the pain and suffering because you bear it for Him. It won't shatter you quite so much to be rejected or disappointed by others when everything you are and have—your identity and hope—is rooted in Christ.

For aid in achieving this, pray the psalms often, asking Our Lady to assist you. I find Psalm 28 particularly helpful. It starts with "To thee, O Lord, I call; my rock" and ends:

The Lord is my strength and my shield;
In him my heart trusts;
So I am helped and my heart exults,
And with my song I give thanks to him.
The Lord is the strength of his people,
He is the saving refuge of his anointed. (Ps 28: 7–9)

Do not expect anyone but Christ to fulfill you.
Do not expect anyone but Christ to save you.

READING LIST

+ The Psalms
+ Walter Joseph Ciszek, S.J., *He Leadeth Me*
+ Walter Joseph Ciszek, S.J., *With God in Russia*

SENTIMENTALITY

Dear Marie Therese,

To dispel any unrealistic expectations you have of religious life and to grow in virtue, you must do battle with sentimentality.

Sentimentality involves acting, thinking, and choosing primarily according to one's emotions or sentiments rather than reason. It is a common and not insignificant fault in young women. Our culture expects and encourages young women to be sentimental.

The problem, however, is that our emotions are an unreliable guide to what is true and good—most especially in the early stages of the spiritual life. When young women act according to what they *feel*, without the corrective restraint of their reason, they often get themselves into trouble. You cannot consistently choose well or wisely if you allow yourself to be governed by your emotions.

Uncorrected sentimentality might deter you from entering religious life, or it may lead you to enter a religious order for which you are ill-suited.

Where can you start in your battle with sentimentality? Place your struggle in the hands of Our Lady. She understands young women because she was one too! She will help you conquer this weakness.

Second, try to develop your understanding of this fault and its remedies. You want to start seeing the ways in which you indulge in sentimentality and how you allow it to influence your choices, actions, and words.

Most young women have read Jane Austen's *Pride and Prejudice*. Her other work, *Sense and Sensibility*, provides a superb portrayal of sentimentality in young women and its harmful consequences. Read and profit from it.

Take time to critically analyze the messages presented to your peers in the music, films, books, and television shows they consume. Too often, romantic feelings and passions are presented as *the* greatest good. Despite our precautions and knowledge, we are subtly influenced by the more prevalent thoughts and errors of our time. Ask God to show you where and in what ways your thinking and choices have been compromised by modern secular culture.

READING LIST

+ Jane Austen, *Sense and Sensibility*

COMPETITION AND HUMILITY

Dear Marie Therese,

Unfortunately, competition and jealousy can be rife among women. Even good women can be tempted to compete with and envy one another. Because jealousy is dark and obviously evil—an overtly shameful thing that feels and looks so unpleasant—it tends to remain hidden. Women compete discretely. Women envy but have trouble admitting it. Women, just like men, can be opportunistic, but they try to conceal it.

Sadly, you will likely find at least some instances of competition, jealousy, envy, and self-preference even in the convent. Religious sisters are not immune to the faults or temptations that the rest of us struggle with. Like all of us, they are broken and imperfect. Yes, they have a spiritually privileged way of life, but they have faults too!

Do not be concerned with others. Focus, rather, on yourself. Where do you see jealousy or competitiveness in *your* thoughts and feelings? Who do *you* compete with? Who makes *you* feel threatened? How does envy influence *your* choices? How does competition with and envy of another handicap *you* from loving that person?

You might, for example, feel pangs of jealousy towards another novice who seems capable of greater prayer, greater cheerfulness, or greater obedience than you. You might find yourself competing with other sisters for the attention and affection of your novice mistress or mother superior. You might find yourself insulted that your cell has less light than sister so-and-so. You might feel happy or smug that your habit is in slightly better condition than that given to someone else. Alternatively, you might feel pride that your habit is a little shabbier than the others'!

A religious sister recently told me that she battles these things by observing them and then naming them. Her motto is to "name it, claim it, and tame it." What is it I am feeling? she asks. What part of "death-to-self" am I resisting? It might be, for example, self-preference. She then gives this fault to God and His mother, asking for their help to overcome it.

You would do well to start training yourself against these vices now before you enter the convent. Like the religious sister I described, ask God to help you see the ways in which you compete and envy. Once you see it, take the fault to Our Lady and Our Lord, and ask them to help you overcome it. Then, calmly and consistently, do the opposite of what you would do if you were to be competitive and jealous.

READING LIST

Inspirational Stories and Cautionary Tales about Priests and Religious

+ William E. Barrett, *The Lilies of the Field* (fiction; inspirational)
+ Georges Bernanos, *The Diary of a Country Priest* (fiction; inspirational)
+ Willa Cather, *Death Comes for the Archbishop* (fiction; inspirational)
+ Sister Cecilia as told to William Brinkley, *The Deliverance*

of Sister Cecilia (autobiographical; inspirational)

+ Graham Greene, *The Power and the Glory* (fiction; inspirational and cautionary)
+ Anne Fontaine, *The Innocents* (French: *Les Innocentes*) (2016 film; inspirational and cautionary)
+ Jean-Pierre Améris, *Marie's Story* (2014 French film; inspirational)
+ Xavier Beauvois, *Of Gods and Men* (2011 French film; inspirational)
+ *The Scarlet and the Black* (1983 film; inspirational)

Prayer for Perseverance

Dear Marie Therese,

It is never too early to start praying for your future vocation as a religious.

We hear of too many souls who have left their vocation to religious life. Good people who, even after solemn vows, cannot persevere. And we hear of too many marriages—seemingly good Catholic marriages with many children—that end in divorce.

Saint John Paul II wrote about the challenge of faithfulness:

> It is easy to be consistent for a day or two. It is difficult and important to be consistent for one's whole life. It is easy to be consistent in the hour of enthusiasm; it is difficult to be so in the hour of tribulation. And only a consistency that lasts throughout the whole of life can be called faithfulness.[179]

We must be humble and realize that we cannot do this alone. We cannot succeed in our vocations—we cannot discern and we cannot become saints—without God's assistance.

Do not underestimate how difficult it is to persevere. Scripture is filled with stories of the faithful falling away—why should we think we are better than Moses, David, or Saint Peter? We are all sons and daughters of Adam and Eve.

---

[179] John Paul II, *The Meaning of Vocation* (New York: Scepter, 1997), 24.

Pray that you remain faithful to your vocation until your death. Pray also for your future religious community. Pray that when you find the right community, this community remains faithful to its charism and traditions as well as the doctrine and praxis of the Church. Pray that it is fruitful. Ask God to send vocations to this order and that its work be ever pleasing to Him.[180]

You might find the following prayer to Our Lady helpful:

Dear Sweet Immaculate Virgin, my mother, Mother of Mercy, please obtain for me, your daughter, the great grace of conversion. Most Holy Mother of God, you know all my sufferings and failings. Through your intercession please cure me of the spiritual and moral deprivations I suffer and in so doing, foster in me a rich interior life, a great love of and obedience to God's will, and form me as a woman, spouse, and mother in your likeness.

I pray, with your help, to remain ever faithful to my vocation and the Catholic faith. Help me to persevere in whatever state of life I am called to. I beg also that these same gifts of perseverance and fidelity be given to my future religious community or spouse.

Oh my Mother, despise not my petitions but in your merciful love, hear and answer me.

---

[180] In the event you do not have a religious vocation, pray that God provides you with a husband who is holy and pure. Ask God to form him as a capable and loving provider and protector who will help you and your children become saints. Pray also that this man be given the grace of perseverance so that he is faithful to you and our Catholic faith for the entirety of his life.

READING LIST

+ Gertrud von le Fort, *The Song at the Scaffold* (fiction)
+ Pierre de Calan, *Cosmas or the Love of God* (fiction)

Quagmires and Endgames

Dear Marie Therese,

Unfortunately, it is not uncommon for souls considering religious life to end up in a discernment quagmire. They won't enter religious life but they can't quite abandon the idea that they are called either. Such souls can toy with the idea of religious life for years on end. They flounder along in a protracted discernment without an endgame in mind.

This is often because they want a clear and definite yes from God before they enter. This is a mistake. Rather, what you should be looking for is a clear and definite no. Ask yourself this:

> Has God made it clear that He is *not* calling me to religious life?

The modern emphasis on the need for an unequivocal affirmative command from God to enter religious life is misdirected and creates unnecessary suffering. God sometimes does make it very clear to certain souls that they are called. He gives them a definitive yes. But not everyone has this experience.

If you have started discernment and made progress in the spiritual life but do not yet know with certainty, make your move and enter religious life. Assume that you *are* called and start your postulancy. This is simply the next stage of your discernment. It is the natural next step.

By doing this, you place your vocation into the hands

of God's Church. God will use His Church to help you discern. In *To Save a Thousand Souls*, Father Brett Brannen gives similar advice to young men discerning whether to enter the seminary:

> If you have made a diligent discernment, but you are still confused and frustrated and don't know what to do next, I recommend this to you: submit it to the Church! Let the bishop decide. You can't go wrong this way. God can't drive a parked car. Move![181]

One of the ways in which your superiors will assess whether you have an authentic vocation to religious life is by observing you throughout the postulancy and novitiate periods to see how you get on. Do you progress? Do you flourish in religious life? What is the fruit?[182]

This approach rests upon what Fr. Brett Brannen calls the "Gamaliel Principle." In Acts 5, a Pharisee by the name of Gamaliel tells the Jews not to kill the Apostles but to release them: "For if this endeavor or this activity is of human origin, it will destroy itself. But if it comes from God, you will not be able to stop it; you may even find yourselves fighting God" (Acts 5:34–39). The Gamaliel Principle, therefore, "states that following Jesus in a radical way, like in the priesthood [or religious life], can most often happen only if God himself is behind it."[183]

---

[181] Brett A. Brannen, *To Save a Thousand Souls: A Guide to Discerning a Vocation to Diocesan Priesthood* (Valdosta, GA: Vianney Vocations, 2010), 185.

[182] Brett Brannen, *A Priest in the Family: A Guide for Parents Whose Sons are Considering Priesthood* (Valdosta, GA: Vianney Vocations, 2014), 36.

[183] Ibid.

And so, rather than asking God over and over again, "Am I called?" recite this prayer instead:

Dear God, please give me the courage and strength to enter the convent. If religious life is not for me, please make it abundantly clear and prevent me from progressing further.

Do Not Delay

Dear Marie Therese,

Once you see that you are or might be called to religious life, do not delay in entering.

I was shocked to hear from a priest that he knew of a number of souls who understand they have a vocation but continually put off entering religious life—choosing instead to tend to this or that, complete a master's degree, enroll in a doctorate, finish some task, take some trip, or wait for some milestone to pass, etc.

Marie Therese, we must pray for these souls! They hurt not only themselves but the Church too.

They remind me of couples who know they are to marry but enter into a protracted and extended courtship or engagement lasting many years. They open themselves to all sorts of dangers and occasions of sin. Worst of all, they risk losing their beloved as a spouse.

In the same way, a soul intended for religious life can also damage or lose her vocation if she isn't careful.

One must also be careful not to spend too long in discernment. Love of God must be manifest in our choices and actions. It is not enough to want God. We must choose God.

Saint Thomas Aquinas warns souls not to take too long in discerning: "In these matters, however, one should not take long deliberation. Wherefore Jerome says: 'Hasten, I pray thee, cut off rather than loosen the rope that holds the boat to shore.'"[184]

If this is something you are struggling with, implore the help of Saint Gabriel of the Sorrowful Virgin—a young Passionist saint who died at age twenty-five. Saint Gabriel put off entering religious life even though he knew he was called by God to be a religious. He wanted to finish college. He wanted to continue a life in which he could read popular novels and attend the dances and social events he so very much enjoyed. He liked expensive, fashionable clothes. He did not want to displease or inconvenience his father. In short, he had a difficult time renouncing his secular dreams and desire for pleasure and success.

Saint Gabriel fell deathly ill not once but twice, and both times promised that he would enter religious life, only to put it off once he recovered. The young saint was able to break with his old way of life only after a locution from Our Lady. As he gazed one day at a beautiful icon of Our Lady, Saint Gabriel heard Mary's voice in his soul: "Francis, why do you linger in the world? Arise, make haste, and become a religious."[185]

If you think you might be called, then decisively cut your ties to the world and enter. As Our Lady said to Saint Gabriel: "Arise, make haste, and become a religious!"

Do not delay!

---

[184] *ST* II-II, q. 189, a. 10.

[185] Camillus Barth, *Boy in a Hurry: The Story of St. Gabriel of the Sorrowful Virgin* (The ECO Press, 1987), 21. Born Francesco Possenti, he changed his name after entering religious life.

READING LIST

+ Camillus Barth, *Boy in a Hurry: The Story of St. Gabriel of the Sorrowful Virgin*

Signs of a Vocation

William Doyle was an Irish Jesuit who died in World War I during the battle of Ypres while tending to wounded and dying soldiers. Before his appointment as a military chaplain he became well known as a preacher and spiritual director throughout Ireland, and wrote a pamphlet on vocations which became a best seller. In this pamphlet, he lists a number of signs which, he says, indicate that someone has a vocation to religious life. You might find it helpful to consider these and prayerfully reflect on whether any of them match with your own experience. Father Doyle notes that "no one need expect to have all these marks."[41]

1. A desire to have a religious vocation, together with the conviction that God is calling you. This desire is generally most strongly felt when the soul is calm, after Holy Communion, and in time of retreat.

2. A growing attraction for prayer and holy things in general, together with a longing for a hidden life and a desire to be more closely united to God.

---

[41] William Doyle, *Vocations* (reprint, CreateSpace Independent Publishing Platform, 2018), 8–9.

3. A hatred of the world, a conviction of its hollowness and insufficiency to satisfy the soul. This feeling is generally strongest in the midst of worldly amusements.

4. A fear of sin, into which it is easy to fall, and a longing to escape from the dangers and temptations of the world.

5. It is sometimes the sign of a vocation when a person fears that God may call them; when he prays not to have it and cannot banish the thought from his mind. If the vocation is sound, it will soon give place to an attraction, though, as Father Lehmkuhl says: "One need not have a natural inclination for the religious life; on the contrary, a divine vocation is compatible with a natural repugnance for the state."

6. To have zeal for souls. To realize something of the value of an immortal soul, and to desire to cooperate in their salvation.

7. To desire to devote our whole life to obtain the conversion of one dear to us.

8. To desire to atone for our own sins or those of others, and to fly from the temptations which we feel too weak to resist.

9. An attraction for the state of virginity.

10. The happiness which the thought of religious life brings, its spiritual helps, its peace, merit and reward.

11. A longing to sacrifice oneself and abandon all for the love of Jesus Christ, and to suffer for His sake.

12. A willingness in one not having any dowry, or much education, to be received in any capacity, is a proof of a real vocation.[42]

Following are some additional considerations I would add to this list of indicators. These indicators focus less on your internal feelings, spiritual impulses, desires, and imagination, and more on gauging the fruit of your preparatory discernment and choices. In other words, they ask you to consider how your soul is responding to various proactive measures (or the lack thereof) undertaken as part of your discernment:

---

[42] Doyle, Vocations.

1. A desire for martyrdom: a desire to give your life for love of God or love of another.

2. An unease or nagging concern, however slight, that you might have a vocation to religious life. Take particular note of this unease or lingering doubt if it occurs while dating someone, entering into an engagement to be married, or doing something otherwise incompatible with religious life. It might also occur while working or when you start or advance in your professional life.

3. An inability, over a period of time, to dispel the idea of religious life or firmly conclude that you are not called. When the question of religious life lingers in your mind and soul, it is an invitation to discern more deeply and take some preparatory steps.

4. Consistent joy, peace, or calm experienced while serving others through spiritual or corporal works of mercy.

5. Consistent joy, peace, or calm experienced when living, working, or interacting with members of a particular religious order. A sense of belonging when you are with a particular order. A sense of being at home when in a particular convent.

6. Evidence of spiritual fruit as a result of your discernment and preparation. This might include progressing with some rapidity through the various stages of prayer, an increase in virtue, or overcoming a particular vice or fault. It can also include spiritual gifts or conversions given to others.

7. Given that vocations are gifted by God not only for the good of the recipient but also for the good of other souls and the benefit of the entire Church, a clear understanding that it will be spiritually better for others and the church as a whole if you enter into religious life.

Finally, I recommend coming back to these lists and reviewing them every couple of months as you prepare and discern. Have any of these signs or characteristics become stronger since you started serious discernment? Or, perhaps there are one or two now that weren't apparent before? If so, it is quite possible that you have a vocation to religious life.